TAKING YOUR PLACE IN CHRIST

by
Mark Hankins

Taking Your Place
In Christ
*Understanding Your Identity
and Inheritance in Him*

Mark Hankins Ministries Publications
Alexandria, Louisiana

Taking Your Place In Christ

ISBN 1-889981-01-X
Copyright © 1996 by Mark Hankins Ministries
Mark Hankins Ministries
P. O. Box 12863
Alexandria, LA 71315

Published by MHM Publications

Fourth printing — 40,000 copies in print.

ACKNOWLEDGMENTS

I would like to give special thanks to those who made this book possible: First of all, to my wonderful wife, Trina and my children, Aaron and Alicia, and my parents, Pastor B.B. and Velma Hankins.

To my outstanding staff who worked many, many hours:

James and Lorene Dewees

Brian and Kimberly Bohrer

Don and Dianne Labro

Tina and Lynn Welch

Chris and Stephanie Welch

Chennette and Donnie Messick

Dewayne and Yvette Soulter

Randy and Becky Goudeau

Mary Scherer

Rachel Graham

Margery and Coy Purkey

Geneva Murphy

CONTENTS

1

FINDING YOUR PLACE IN CHRIST

A traveling man entered a town, looking for a certain address. He pulled into a driveway of a home where a little boy was playing in the front yard, to ask for directions. He rolled down his window and called to the little boy, "Where am I?" The little boy answered, "<u>Right there you are!</u>"

Many times in life we search for answers and direction and God shows us in His Word a simple, "Right there you are!" Understanding where you are has everything to do with finding your destiny and direction in life.

When you go into a large shopping mall, a map is usually posted, identifying the different stores that are available on each level. It still may be difficult, however, to find your way around without a note on the map that says, "<u>You are here.</u>"

Understanding the New Birth and who you are *in Christ* begins with several "right there you are" and "you are here" Scriptures. A good place to begin is 2 Corinthians 5:17: *Therefore if any man be in Christ, he is a new creature: old things are passed away; behold, all things are become new.*

Another Scripture is 2 Corinthians 5:21: *For he hath made him to be sin for us, who knew no sin; that we might be made the righteousness of God in him.* Another identification Scripture is Colossians 2:9,10: *For in him dwelleth all the fulness of the Godhead bodily. And ye are complete in him, which is the head of all principality and power.*

There are more than 130 in *Christ* Scriptures that locate who you are and what you have in Him. One of my favorites is 2 Corinthians 2:14: *Now thanks be unto God, which always causeth us to triumph in Christ, and maketh manifest the savour of his knowledge by us in every place.*

You accept the integrity of God's Word and boldly declare, "I am who God says I am. I have what God says I have. And I can do what God says I can do." Right there you are — *In Christ!*

I am a preacher's kid. When I was growing up, we were called PK's. My dad and mom pastor a Full Gospel church in West Columbia, Texas. They have pastored The Christian Center for more than forty-two years. The church has grown to be the largest church in West Columbia and the largest Full Gospel church in the area.

When my parents first moved to West Columbia, I was only a year old and my older brother, Mike, was four. Mom was sick and mentally tormented for the first two years in West Columbia. Dad not only pastored the church, but he had the pressure of all the family responsibilities. Then he began to have heart trouble. During this same time, while I was playing outside one day with Mike, I stuck my thumb into a bicycle chain and cut off my thumb. I don't remember ever having two thumbs! The church was small and struggling, and we were poor. It was a tough time for us.

In the middle of this struggle, a man gave my dad some books on the authority of the believer, the integrity of God's Word and who you are *in Christ*. Dad began to read and study the material, and he gained new understanding of God's Word.

Psalm 119:130 says, *The entrance of thy words giveth light; it giveth understanding unto the simple.* Thank God for His Word!

Dad began to speak the Word to Mom and had her repeat it

after him. She began to say, "I am who God says I am. I have what God says I have. I can do what God says I can do!" As they saw who they were *in Christ* and spoke the Word, faith arose in their hearts, and they knew that victory was theirs in every area of their lives.

IT'S NOT NECESSARY
UNLESS IT'S NECESSARY

As I grew up in church, there were some "unusual" services. Sometimes while we sang, Mom would begin to praise God rather exuberantly and shout, "Hallelujah! Hallelujah! Hallelujah!" With glory and joy on her countenance, she would shout "Woooooo!" and run around the church! Dad was a little more dignified! After Mom would run, Dad would say, "Now, some of you don't think that is necessary, and it's not necessary unless it's necessary!" While the congregation was trying to figure out what he had said, Mom and others who had joined her would finish their rejoicing!

When I became a teenager, this was very embarrassing to me. When we were encouraged to bring visitors to church, I would say, "I'm not going to bring my friends to this church...I would never live it down."

Then one day a friend of mine showed up in our church. I certainly hadn't invited him! As soon as I saw him, I went and sat by him and began to pray, "O God, please don't let this be a wild service, and please don't let my mother run." That's a dangerous prayer!

MY MOTHER RUNS

About that time, people began to sense the power of God and started rejoicing. The Holy Spirit fell on the entire place. My friend's eyes got big. I tried to comfort him and tell him everything would be all right. Then my mother began to say,

"Hallelujah! Hallelujah! Hallelujah!" I thought, "Oh, no, she's revving up her engine." Sure enough, I heard a "Woooooo!" and she started running around the church.

I put my head down, and my friend asked, "Who is that woman?" I said, "I have no idea! We get all kinds of unusual people in here!" I made sure he never came to my house. I was ashamed of the power of God, and I had little understanding or appreciation of the pit my mother had come out of.

Psalm 40:2,3 says: *He brought me up also out of an horrible pit, and out of the miry clay, and set my feet upon a rock, and established my goings. And he hath put a new song in my mouth, even praise unto our God....*

I did not understand the magnitude of my mother's deliverance until I was seventeen and running from God. Coming home from a party with a backslidden friend, we had an automobile accident that totalled several cars, yet we walked away without a scratch. My backslidden friend said, "If your mom wasn't praying, we would have been killed." I agreed.

SATAN HATH DESIRED TO HAVE YOU

When I got home, Mom was sitting in a rocking chair. She spoke the words that Jesus spoke to Peter: *...Satan hath desired to have you, that he might sift you as wheat: but I have prayed for thee, that thy faith fail not: and when thou art converted, strengthen thy brethren* (Luke 22:31,32).

Although good changes had begun in my life, not long after the automobile accident, three friends and I ended up in the county jail. I called Mom from the jail, and she said, "Your dad has church tonight (it was a Wednesday night), so just prop your feet up and stay awhile!" After church, Dad and four deacons came to the jail and put up bond for me so I could go home.

After that incident, I sold my '55 Chevrolet and that sobered me up for a while!

Within a few months I was in Tanzania, East Africa, with missionary Ralph Hagemeier. How that happened was a mystery to me! I had a desire in my heart to serve God and one day do mission work in Africa, but I seemed to stay in trouble. (Some say preachers' kids are so bad because they hang around with deacons' kids!)

ARRESTED BY GOD

One Sunday God had a surprise for me. I was sitting on the back row, cutting up, and God arrested me. An unannounced guest speaker, F. E. Ward, came to church that Sunday. Brother Ward was a big, stocky preacher. You never knew when he was going to show up, and that Sunday I was not prepared for what was about to happen.

Since our church believed in the baptism of the Holy Spirit and the gifts of the Spirit, the supernatural was often in manifestation. Sometimes preachers would call someone out and give them a word from the Lord. Usually, I would know when they were coming, and I would repent of all my sins in the foyer before I came into the auditorium.

I knew the Bible said that if we asked God to forgive us, He would forgive and even forget our transgressions. I thought, "If God forgets it, then He can't tell that preacher, and that preacher can't tell the whole church."

But that Sunday I was sitting on the back row with my backslidden friends when Brother Ward went to the platform and said he felt led to do something. He pointed to the back and said, "I want the pastor's son to come to the front."

I was shocked! My friends made a comment, "You're a dead

duck now!" As I got up and headed down the aisle, I began to repent under my breath: "O God, forgive me of my sins! Please don't tell that preacher what I've been doing. If You tell him and he tells everybody, my dad will kill me." All the blood drained from my face, and I was afraid and embarrassed as I stood in front of the whole church. I was only seventeen, but I thought my life had come to an end!

I fully expected God to bring out a giant flyswatter and squash me in front of the whole church. I expected a voice from heaven to say, "Let this young man be an example to the rest of you in this church. Put twelve stones on this greasy spot, and tell your kids about it!"

Instead, I heard the voice of F. E. Ward say, "Sit down on the altar." As I sat down, he began to speak to me under the inspiration of the Holy Spirit. As he spoke to me about God's plan and purpose for my life, the presence and love of God overwhelmed me, and I began to cry.

I surrendered my life to Jesus again, and my heart was changed by the love of God. Rev. Ward then took an offering for me so I could spend the summer in Africa. Believe me, my life took a dramatic turn from that moment!

I've often thought I should write a country western song called, "Jesus Loved the Hell out of Me." I don't mean to be crude or irreverent, but that is exactly what happened to me. I like to say, "I went to school, and they tried to educate the 'hell' out of me. I went to church, and they tried to preach the 'hell' out of me. I went to jail, and they tried to rehabilitate the 'hell' out of me. I went home, and Dad tried to beat the 'hell' out of me. I went to Jesus, and He loved the hell out of me." I am a living testimony that the love of God is the greatest force on earth.

I AM WHO GOD SAYS I AM

Dad's preaching and Mom's praying and running around the

church began to make sense to me. I started studying the Scriptures that showed me my Redemption *in Christ*. I daily meditated on who I am *in Christ*. I would say, "I am who God says I am. I have what God says I have. And I can do what God says I can do."

The power of God's Word started a work in me, and I began to understand who I am *in Christ*. And that's where victory begins — "Right where you are!"

Today, Mom still runs around the church, which is much larger now. There are a lot more educated and prosperous people in their congregation, but she still says, "Hallelujah! Hallelujah! Hallelujah!" She still shouts "Whooooo," and runs around the church. The only difference is, now I shout and run with her! *...I am not ashamed of the gospel of Christ: for it is the power of God unto salvation to every one that believeth...* (Romans 1:16).

SHOUT IT OUT

The company that makes Shout detergent advertises their product: "For those tough stains, you have to Shout them out!" I couldn't agree more. Make sure you know what you are shouting about and let it rip!

Smith Wigglesworth said, "Some people would be giants in faith if they just had a shout." Faith shouts while the walls are still standing. He also said, "You need to see how wonderful you are in God and how helpless you are without Him."

The truth is, everything changes when you understand who you are *in Christ* and when you begin to act like the Bible is true!

2

THE SECRET PLACE

And he said, Thou canst not see my face: for there shall no man see me, and live.

And the Lord said, Behold, there is a place by me, and thou shalt stand upon a rock.

Exodus 33:20,21

Moses is getting in on the secret of the power and authority of God. God told Moses, "There is a place I want to take you to, Moses. It's right by Me, and you are going to stand upon a Rock." Jesus is that Rock!

Moses is getting in on the secret of God's Plan of Redemption — that man belongs at the right hand of God, meaning *in His presence.* That's what Paul said in Ephesians 2:5,6:

Even when we were dead in sins, hath quickened us together with Christ, (by grace ye are saved;)

And hath raised us up together, and made us sit together in heavenly places in Christ Jesus:

When you were born again, you didn't go from being a lost worm to a saved worm! If you are saved, you are *in Christ*, and you are *identified with Him.* You are raised with Christ and seated together with Him. (We will discuss your identity *in Christ* in more detail in Chapter 6.)

Let's look at Exodus 33:22,23:

And it shall come to pass, while my glory passeth by, that I will put thee in a clift of the rock, and will cover thee with my hand while I pass by:

And I will take away mine hand, and thou shalt see my back parts: but my face shall not be seen.

God told Moses, "There is a place by Me for you. You are going to stand on a Rock." (That Rock is Jesus and the Plan of Redemption.)

Moses wasn't just going to stand on the Rock. God put him in the cleft of the Rock, which means, "I'm going to carve out a niche in this Rock and put you inside of the Rock. Now you can see my glory and my goodness and understand who I Am."

GETTING INTO POSITION

Several years ago, I heard that NASA had launched a satellite that was absolutely useless into outer space. It was a communications satellite that could not receive or transmit because it was in the wrong orbit. Investors were very concerned because they had already spent $150 million on this project. If the satellite were operating properly, it had a potential of $2 billion. Yet it was worthless.

Somehow it had ended up in the wrong orbit. For it to work properly, they would have to attach some rockets to it and move it to its proper orbit. I don't understand much about outer space technology, so that didn't make sense to me. I thought that if you could just get the thing out of this atmosphere and into outer space, it ought to work right. Whether it makes sense to me or not doesn't matter; the thing still won't receive or transmit.

Since the investment was $150 million, and the potential is $2 billion, something had to change for this satellite to receive and transmit. They were able to fire some rockets attached to the sides of the satellite and move it into its proper orbit. As soon as it was moved into place, it began to receive and transmit, and its potential was realized.

MAKING ADJUSTMENTS

Finding your place *in Christ* is the key to receiving from God and transmitting His power. Sometimes you think just because you got born again, everything ought to work right. You think, "I'm out there; why don't things work right for me?"

The new birth is the launching power that gets you into the realm of God; however, there are other changes that must be made in your thinking and speaking that will enable you to receive and transmit the glory of God. You may not be receiving and transmitting because you need to make some adjustments. You need to get in the right orbit to receive and transmit. Not only do you need to be in the right place, but God needs you to be in your place to do His will. He is working in you both to will and to do of His good pleasure (Philippians 2:13).

He has some rockets to help you move into position to see His glory. He has given His Word, the Holy Spirit, and the fivefold ministry to help you make adjustments. It takes some changes to get the glory, and it takes the glory to get some changes. You are being changed so you can fit and function in the proper orbit and realize your potential *in Christ*.

Throughout the Bible, we see God moving men and women into the proper orbit to be used by Him. God is constantly working with people to change their thinking, speaking, and acting to open up the miraculous for them. Not only does God want to bless you; He wants to make you a blessing. You can see this in the life of Abraham as he demonstrates faith that pleases God. Abraham had to do some "moving" or make some adjustments so he could receive and transmit. Today, you also must be aware of what time it is. It is harvest time, and God is showing you your place *in Christ* and setting you in your place for world harvest.

3

FINDING YOUR PLACE IN THE ROCK

I was raised in church. We never voted on whether or not we would go. My daddy said, "This is not a democracy. This is a dictatorship." We didn't always like it, but I'm glad now that he made us go. We went to church every time the doors were open. If they had a two-week meeting, we were there every night for two weeks. I used to hear the congregation sing, "Rock of Ages, cleft for me, let me hide myself in thee." I never had a clue as to what they were singing about until I was nineteen years old.

One day I went to my daddy's church and began to pray. After two and a half hours of praying in the Holy Ghost, the Spirit of God fell on me and God said, "There is a place for you by Me. I want to show you your place."

I had a vision. The Lord took me up into the heavenly places, and He said, "This is your place." There was a big Rock. He said, "This is your place — right by Me!"

In His presence I experienced joy, blessing, and victory like I had never known. I didn't know about Exodus 33 until several years later. God had spoken to me exactly what He spoke to Moses: ...*There is a place by me, and thou shalt stand upon a rock.* . . . (v. 21).

YOUR PLACE BY THE FATHER

There is a place by the Father, and that place is *in Christ* Jesus.

When you are born again, you move out of the devil's territory, and you are relocated in a new place *in Christ.*

When I had the vision, God also said to me: "I have had your place by Me reserved for you even before you were born. I prepared it ahead of time. Find that place and get in it. There is deliverance, healing, prosperity, victory, and blessing in that place."

Find your place by the Father. Live in that place. Don't let Hollywood tell you who you are, where your place is, and how to dress, look, or act. Don't let people shape you. Get in the presence of God, and let Him shape you.

He will shape your mind, your life, and your future. Don't let your past failures or weaknesses shape you. In prayer, in the name of Jesus and by the blood of Jesus, make your way into your place by the Father.

Psalm 91:1,2 says:

He that dwelleth in the secret place of the most High shall abide under the shadow of the Almighty.

I will say of the Lord, He is my refuge and my fortress: my God; in him will I trust.

Psalm 91 is a great insurance policy! The company will never go broke. We're to live in that secret place.

Psalm 32:7 says, "Thou art my hiding place; thou shalt preserve me from trouble; thou shalt compass me about with songs of deliverance."

YOUR PLACE IN CHRIST

Climb into the secret place by the Father, and you will hear somebody singing songs of deliverance. Hallelujah!

When Saul met Jesus on the road to Damascus, the first thing he said to Jesus was, "Who art thou, Lord?" (Acts 9:5). The second thing he said to Jesus was, *Lord, what wilt thou have me to do?* (v. 6).

Saul, who became Paul, then spent the rest of his life finding out who Jesus was and doing what He wanted him to do. He coined a phrase that is the signature of all of his letters: *in Christ.*

Very seldom do people use this phrase, *in Christ,* but Paul said, *In Christ you are a new creation. In Him you are the righteousness of God. In Him you are triumphant. In Him you are blessed. In Him you are redeemed. In Him you have a heritage — an identity and an inheritance!*

You will look a lot better *in Christ* than you do outside of Him. So what do you need to do? Get on the Rock, climb into the Rock, and *in Him* the glory of God will pass by. *In Him* you will be changed. *In Him* is revelation. *In Him* the goodness of God will come to your house.

If you are outside of Jesus Christ, and you want to be *in Him,* pray with me right now:

Father, I want to find my place in Christ by You, which You ordained for me before I was formed in the womb.

I acknowledge Jesus Christ as your Son, and I believe He was crucified, buried, resurrected, and ascended to your right hand, Father, paying for my redemption, liberty, health, prosperity, and eternal life with His shed blood.

I renounce every work of darkness, and I receive You now, Jesus, as my personal Lord and Savior.

Thank You for empowering me with Your Spirit, Who will teach, guide and lead me into my place in You. Amen.

4

UNDERSTANDING REDEMPTION
GOD'S MASTERPIECE

God did "in Christ" what He wanted to do in every man. God deposited all that He has "in Christ" and then he put us "in Christ."

The Bible is the story of man's Redemption. All 66 books contain pictures of God's plan and purpose to restore man to Himself. So Jesus can be found in every book of the Bible. The Bible is about Jesus, our Redeemer, and His work.

The Louvre in Paris, France, is famous for its display of the world's greatest art collection. It covers more than 40 acres and exhibits many of the world's greatest art treasures. The Louvre has about eight miles of galleries and contains more than a million works of art. While preaching in Paris, I had one day to do some sightseeing. On the way to the Louvre, my minister friend told me that there were more than 400,000 masterpieces to see. If I spent four seconds in front of each one, it would take me three months to go through the Louvre. Since I did not have that much time, when I entered I headed for the information desk to find out where Leonardo da Vinci's world-famous masterpiece, The Mona Lisa, was. We headed right for The Mona Lisa and spent extra time there. If you see all the other paintings and sculptures and miss The Mona Lisa, you have missed the most important work of art. The same is true of the Bible. It contains the world's greatest collection of God's works of art. However, if you see all the beautiful pictures in the Word of God and miss God's greatest masterpiece; then you really have missed the Bible.

FIRST IMPORTANCE

The death, burial, and resurrection of Jesus is the center of the Gospel. Paul says in I Corinthians 15:1-4 that he preached the Gospel, and then he says, "For I delivered unto you first of all that which I also received, how that Christ died for our sins according to the scriptures; And that he was buried, and that he rose again the third day according to the scriptures."

Paul says, "First of all" I delivered unto you. The Revised Standard Version translates it, "as of first importance." The New English Bible says, "First and foremost, I handed on to you the facts which had been imparted to me." Weymouth's translation says, "Before all else. The matter of 'first importance' is what God did for us *in Christ* Jesus in the great Plan of Redemption."

God's masterpiece happened "*in Christ*." What God did for us in the death, burial, and resurrection of Christ is "the masterpiece." You must see what happened from the cross to the throne. There is the greatest display of love, wisdom, power, and righteousness in the history of time and eternity. The Holy Spirit will help you to see. He is your Tour Guide as you study Redemption.

Redemption is an accomplished fact "*in Christ*." Jesus said, *You shall know the truth and the truth shall make you free* (John 8:32). The truth will not help you if you do not "know" it. You must see what God has done for you. In John 16:13, Jesus called the Holy Spirit the "Spirit of Truth." God wants you to be free. He has given His Holy Spirit to show you the things of Christ. The simple definition of Redemption is: Freedom through the payment of a price. The dictionary defines redeem as: to buy back; to repurchase; to get back; to recover; to ransom; to payoff (a mortgage or note); to liberate from captivity; to deliver; to reclaim. The apostle Paul says in I Timothy 2:6, "Who gave Himself a ransom for all, to be testified in due time." Other translations say:

Plain English — Who gave himself as the price of freedom for all men...

Adams — ...gave Himself as a ransom payment for all sorts of persons.

Translator's — He gave himself to set all men free.

Jesus gave Himself as our ransom payment. He purchased our freedom.

Faith begins by knowing Redemption facts. God paid the price for you "*in Christ*" 2,000 years ago. As the old Gospel song says, "Jesus paid it all." So Christianity does not begin with something you do but with something that has been done for you *in Christ*. Everything Jesus did in His death and resurrection was done for you or, as some translations say, "in our behalf."

If everything Jesus did was "for you," it is set to the credit of your account. You could say Jesus gets the "Glory" for everything that has been done, but you get the "credit" because He was acting in your behalf. One of my favorite scriptures is Hebrews 9:12, "Neither by the blood of goats and calves, but by his own blood he entered once into the holy place, having obtained eternal redemption for us." One translation says, "...secured our permanent deliverance" (Goodspeed). I like that! Think about it! Jesus has secured our permanent deliverance. That is a powerful statement!

Satan's dominion has been broken over mankind "permanently" because of what Christ has done. Redemption is not a temporary thing that must be added to by man or replaced later by something more effective. The Amplified Bible says, "...a complete redemption, an everlasting release." A complete redemption covers everything. An "everlasting release" means it lasts forever. God has left nothing out.

All that man needs is supplied *in Christ*. The past, present, and future have been taken care of. The spirit, soul, and body have been taken care of — all because of what Jesus has done "for us."

That means you are not trying to get it or struggling to get it. Jesus got it for you, so it is yours. You have it now. Redemption is an accomplished fact *in Christ*.

The definition of Redemption is "deliverance or freedom through the payment of a price." Jesus paid the price for your release. Look at several *hath* scriptures that the apostle Paul wrote in his letters. Christ "hath" redeemed you from the curse of the law (Galatians 3:13). God *hath* qualified you for your inheritance (Colossians 1:12). He *hath* delivered you from the power of darkness and *hath* translated you into the kingdom of His dear Son (Colossians 1:13). He *hath* blessed you with every spiritual blessing *in Christ* (Ephesians 1:3). These "hath" scriptures show that Jesus *hath* — past tense — paid the price, and the prisoner must be released. Man is literally held captive by sin, Satan, sickness, fear, poverty, guilt, and many other things. Jesus paid the price for your freedom. Jesus said, *You shall know the truth and the truth shall make you free* (John 8:32). Again, He whom the Son sets free is free indeed (John 8:36). Again, in the first message that Jesus preached, He said He would *preach deliverance to the captives* (Luke 4:18). Beck's translation says, "...he sent me to announce to prisoners, 'You are free.' "

Here Jesus is not talking about his "jail ministry." There are a lot of people who are prisoners who are not in a county jail or a federal prison. A prison ministry is a great ministry, but there are many people held captive who are not behind "steel" bars; they are behind "real" bars. Only Jesus can bring deliverance. Only the power of the Gospel can bring freedom. Your release from prison has been accomplished through a price that was paid "in your behalf." In other words, this is not an illegal "jail break." Your

Redemption was legally purchased through the blood of Jesus. His death and resurrection has established a new, universal fact for every man. Jesus purchased your freedom. That means the prison doors of Satan, sin, and sickness are open, and the prisoner is free — Legally! The prisoner does not have to sneak out some dark night. He can walk out in the daylight, because he has a legal release. God has not given you an illegal Redemption. God is righteous, and He has righteously effected your release.

You were prisoners, but now you are free, and you do not have to hide or sneak around the rest of your lives in fear. You have been released, made righteous, and given eternal life — all legally.

I Peter 1:18,19 says "Ye were not redeemed with silver and gold....but with the precious blood of Christ...." No amount of money could buy your release from Satan, sin, or the past. Only the blood of Jesus was legal payment for your freedom. If Jesus paid so high a price for your release, you should not remain behind the bars. The prison door is open. You can simply walk out when you see what Christ has done for you.

A LEGAL RELEASE

It is not like you were prisoners and someone visited you and gave you a file, a little saw, or something else that you could use to try to get out on your own effort. Night after night you would stay up late and secretly file away on the steel bars, hoping not to get caught. After months and years of work, you would finally break a few bars and try to get away. Then you would run, and the dogs and the guards would be chasing you as you ran through the swamp, only to be captured again and returned to the same old prison. That is not a picture of God's release! That is the struggle of mans programs to try to get free. The Gospel of Christ is the power of God. God has released you by His power working *in Christ* in your behalf. The prison door is open! No filing. No sneaking. No running. No swamps. No dogs. It is not your effort. It is God's gift to every man "*in Christ.*" Christ "hath" redeemed you. You can walk out of your bondage into glorious liberty. You are legally released. Hold your head up high, and boldly walk out in Jesus Name!

Let's look closely at Galatians 3:13: *Christ hath redeemed us from the curse of the law, being made a curse for us: for it is written, Cursed is every one that hangeth on a tree.* There are three simple yet powerful statements made in that one verse.

The first fact is that you are redeemed. The second is what you are redeemed from: the curse of the law. The third is what you were redeemed by: Christ was made a curse for us. In other words, Christ took your curse so you could go free. One translation says, *The law put a curse on us.* But Christ took away that curse. He changed places with you. Deaf's translation says, "Christ put himself under that curse...." The Hayman's translation says, *Christ it was who redeemed us from that curse of the law, by receiving our curse on his own person.* Weymouth's translation says, "Christ has purchased our freedom." Jesus paid much too high a price for your freedom for you to stay bound. It is an insult to God for you to stay in prison when Jesus paid the price for your release. Satan cannot hold you; sin cannot hold you; the past cannot hold you. Back to our first fact: YOU ARE REDEEMED!

Next Paul tells you what you are redeemed from. It is true that you will one day go to heaven, and that will be a great day. However, someone said, "I don't just need help in the sweet by-and-by; I need help in the nasty now-and-now." Galatians 3:13 says you are redeemed from the "curse of the law."

To see what the curse of the law is, you need to turn to Deuteronomy 28. The curses are listed in verses 15 through 68. That list includes everything from sickness and poverty to disaster in the family and the nation. The curse includes everywhere you go, everything you do, and everybody you are with. Under the curse, you are a traveling contagious disaster spiritually, mentally, and physically. But Christ hath redeemed you from that curse. He paid the price for your freedom. Even now the curse is broken. Jesus demonstrated this Gospel by healing the sick and setting the captives free in this world. The same Gospel produced the same results in the book of Acts. In Acts 14:7, Paul preached the Gospel, and the crippled man at Lystra received faith to be healed as he heard the message. *Faith cometh by hearing and hearing by the Word of God* (Romans 10:17). Paul said with a loud voice, *Stand upright on thy feet*, and he leaped and walked. The people thought Paul healed the man, but it was simply the demonstration of the power of the Gospel. The curse of the law has been broken — not for just a few select individuals but for "whosoever" will hear and believe the Gospel. The center of the Gospel is what God has done for you *"in Christ."* Christ hath redeemed you. Not just when you get to heaven. The curse of the law is broken today for any man or woman who is *"in Christ."*

You can see the reverse of the curse by reading Deuteronomy 28:1-13. All these blessings shall come on you and overtake you. You are blessed in the city, field, family, body, business, and you are *the head and not the tail, above only and not beneath.*

Christ hath redeemed you. The Gospel is the good news that man has been given eternal life through Jesus Christ. That life is the very life of God imparted to His children. It is overcoming life...reigning life...victorious life...blessing life...healing life...not just for when you get to heaven. It is heaven's life flowing in you in this world.

The Gospel of Christ is the power of God unto salvation to everyone who believes (Romans 1:16). Someone said if you think you need more power, you really just need more Gospel. The Gospel is the Power of God. The word "Gospel" means, "Glad

Tidings" or "Good News." The Gospel is where God has released His power for the purpose of producing salvation.

God has targeted His power at man's deepest needs — spirit, soul, and body. God knows the root of your problems, and He has effectually focused His power there. Everything Satan has done in Adam, God has reversed *in Christ*. The word salvation has a fivefold meaning: deliverance, healing, safety, preservation, and soundness. This is not just a heaven message; but it is an earth message as well. It is not just something for later; this is a "Now" message.

Colossians 1:14 says, "In whom we have redemption through his blood even the forgiveness of sins." Notice "we have redemption" *in Christ*. The Living Bible says, "who bought our freedom with his own blood." Goodspeed says, "by whom we have been ransomed from captivity."

Again, in Ephesians 1:7, Paul says by the Holy Spirit, "In whom we have redemption through his blood, the forgiveness of sins, according to the riches of his grace." Other translations say:

> Barclay: *It is in and through Christ and the sacrifice of His life that we have been liberated.*

> Barth: *...through the shedding of His blood we possess freedom in Him.*

> Jordan: *For it was by this one's supreme sacrifice that we got our emancipation.*

> Beck: *who bought us with his blood to forgive our sins and set us free.*

The center of the Gospel is the death, burial, and resurrection of Christ. After His resurrection, Jesus told the disciples, *Go into all the world and preach the Gospel to every creature.* There are ten messages recorded in the Book of Acts that show us what they understood the Gospel to be — five messages by the apostle Peter and five by the apostle Paul.

In each message, the central point is that Jesus died, He was buried, but He arose from the dead. He is alive! This is the center of the Gospel. The disciples knew what those events had produced for every man. The power that God released in the resurrection of Christ is contained in the message.

Someone said that the death, burial, and resurrection of Christ are "Eternal God Events." We give them a date and place because they are historical events. But they are more than just "history." They are supernatural, eternal God events, and they can be visited at any point in time as though they were happening right then. The same power that God released in the events themselves is in the message. The Gospel contains the power that God released "*in Christ*" 2,000 years ago.

The Gospel produces faith. The Word of God is a living thing. Christ hath redeemed you! The Gospel is not the good news that God "can" help you. It is not the good news that God "wants" to help you. It is the "Good News" that God "has already" helped you *in Christ*. The price has been paid, and the prisoner is free. The curse of sin and Satan has been broken by the mighty Name of Jesus. His blood still speaks of your Redemption today.

In the apostle Paul's letters to the Church, there is a network of revelation concerning who Christ is and what He has done. I call it Paul's System of Truth from Weymouth's translation of Romans 6:17: "But thanks be to God that though you were once in thraldom to Sin, you have now yielded a hearty obedience to that system of truth in which you have been instructed."

This "System of Truth" can be found throughout Paul's letters. These things are interrelated and form a Redemption network centered on the death and resurrection of Christ with the restoration of man as the object. There are eight points in Paul's System of Truth:

1. Man on three dimensions: spirit, soul, body

2. Identification with Adam

3. Man's condition in Adam

4. What happened to Jesus from the Cross to the Throne

5. Identification with Christ

6. Who we are and what we have NOW *in Christ*

7. What Jesus is doing for us at the right hand of God

8. How to develop to spiritual maturity

I have studied "Paul's System of Truth" since I was about seventeen years old. I still do not tire of it, and I have never completed it. I will only touch on this briefly here. (You can order my book *Paul's System of Truth*.) Romans 6:17-18, the apostle Paul says this: *But God be thanked, that ye were the servants of sin, but you have obeyed from the heart that form of doctrine which was delivered you. And being then made free from sin, you became the servants of righteousness.*

Not only are you free from sin, but here it says that you become a servant or a slave of righteousness. How did that happen? Paul says, "You obeyed the form of doctrine that was delivered you."

Many people say, "Well, doctrine is legalism, or doctrine is denominationalism, or doctrine is going to lock me in." However, the apostle Paul says, *All scripture is given by inspiration of God, and is profitable...for instruction in righteousness: That the man of God may be perfect* (II Timothy 3:16,17). Weymouth's translation says, *You obeyed the system of truth in which you were instructed.* So doctrine is a system of truth.

What is a system? A system is a group of items that are interrelated and interdependent upon each other. They cannot stand alone. They must work together. That's a system. For example, there are several television networks such as ABC, NBC, and CBS.

If you're an affiliate of ABC, NBC, or CBS, you must show the same thing on your affiliate station as they show, or you cannot be in their network. Networks work together. Computer systems have network. The universe has a solar system. The human body has a nervous system and digestive system. The simplest illustration of a system is a chain. A chain is a group of links that are interdependent upon each other for the strength of the whole. Not any one link can be a chain; all the links are dependent upon each other. In Paul's System of Truth, the eight points are the are eight links which center in Redemption. In Romans 6:17, Paul says, *You obeyed a system of truth that you were instructed in.*

Whatever Paul taught in Rome, he taught in Colossae, he taught in Ephesus, he taught in Corinth, he taught in Thessalonica, and he wrote in his letter to the Hebrews. His system of truth contains the revelation of what God did *in Christ*—in His death, burial and Resurrection, and its effect upon you. This is something Paul covers more thoroughly than the other Bible writers.

PROCLAMATION, DEMONSTRATION, EXPLANATION

The four Gospels — Matthew, Mark, Luke and John — are a proclamation of the Gospel. The Book of Acts is a demonstration of the Gospel. Paul's epistles are an explanation of the Gospel. We must have the Gospel of Christ in all three forms: proclamation, demonstration, and explanation.

One of the apostle Paul's assignments was to write a Holy Spirit-inspired explanation of the Gospel of Christ. Paul's revelation tells us the necessity of the crucifixion of Christ. He tells us what happened in the unseen, or in the spirit. The four Gospels tell what man saw and Paul's epistles tell us what God saw. Paul tells us what happened in God's economy when Jesus died and was raised from the dead. Paul tells what happened when Jesus ascended into heaven and secured our redemption with his blood.

The four Gospels are a photograph of Redemption and Paul's epistles are an X ray. You can see things in an X ray of an individual that you cannot see in a photograph. Both of these pictures are necessary. The Gospel is multifaceted and meets every need. (I cover this subject more in detail in my book, *Paul's System of Truth.*)

UNDERSTANDING RIGHTEOUSNESS

Understanding righteousness and understanding Redemption are essential to your faith working mightily. Righteousness simply means right standing with God. The main theme of the Book of Romans is righteousness. The apostle Paul begins by saying that the Gospel of Christ is fundamentally a revelation of righteousness.

For I am not ashamed of the gospel of Christ: for it is the power of God unto salvation to every one that believeth; to the Jew first, and also to the Greek. For therein is the righteousness of God revealed from faith to faith: as it is written, The just shall live by faith.

Romans 1:16,17

Righteousness is living in a state of Divine favor or being pleasing, accepted, or approved by God. Righteousness enables you to stand in God's presence without a sense of sin, shame, or guilt. Righteousness is a gift. Romans 5:17 says, *For if by one man's offence death reigned by one; much more they which receive the abundance of grace and the gift of righteousness shall reign in life by one, Jesus Christ.* The Gospel is a revelation of how God makes man righteous. Second Corinthians 5:21 not only tells you what you have but how you got it. *For He hath made him to be sin for us who knew no sin, that we might be made the righteousness of God in him.* Jesus took your sinful condition that you could receive His righteous condition. He took your place so you could have His place.

37

SUBSTITUTION, IDENTIFICATION, UNION

Everything Jesus did, He did for you, so it is set to the credit of your account, as though you did it. This is the progression from substitution, identification, and union with Christ.

When someone is born again, He is a new creature *in Christ Jesus*; old things are passed away and everything is new, (II Cor. 5:17). However, God would not make an unrighteous new creature. If you are saved, you must be righteous. Romans 10:9,10 says, *That if thou shalt confess with thy mouth the Lord Jesus, and shalt believe in thine heart that God hath raised Him from the dead, thou shalt be saved. For with the heart man believeth unto righteousness: and with the mouth confession is made unto salvation.* Romans 4:25 says, *Who was delivered for our offences, and was raised again for our justification.* When Jesus was raised from the dead, you were justified or declared righteous. You could say that Jesus was not raised from the dead until you were declared righteous. The penalty for sin was paid in full and God declared you righteous. This is the reason the Gospel is Good News to every person.

Paul says it this way in Romans 3:21-26:

But now the righteousness of God without the law is manifested, being witnessed by the law and the prophets; Even the righteousness of God which is by faith of Jesus Christ unto all and upon all them that believe: for there is no difference:

For all have sinned, and come short of the glory of God; Being justified freely by His grace through the redemption that is in Christ Jesus:

Whom God set forth to be a propitiation through faith in his blood, to declare his righteousness for the remission of sins that are past, through the forbearance of God;

To declare, I say, at this time his righteousness: that he might be just, and the justifier of him which believeth in Jesus.

Righteousness is yours through faith in the precious blood of

Jesus. God has not only forgiven the sinner, but He has made him His very own righteousness. He has not only forgiven the one who believes in Jesus, but He has forgotten that he has ever done anything wrong, (Isaiah 43:25,26). You are not only forgiven, but you have been recreated with God's own righteousness imparted to you. We have been recreated in Righteousness.

Jesus has given you His standing with the Father God. Jesus has let you share His place with God. *In Christ* is your place of righteousness. In Him you are free from the power, control, and effects of sin. In Him you have confidence in the presence of God. In Him and by faith in His blood you have boldness not only before God but before your Adversary the devil, who comes to accuse you. In Him you are free from guilt and shame. In Him you are free from inferiority and unworthiness.

You can grow in faith, love, and holiness, but not in righteousness. You can never get any more righteous than the moment you are born again and washed in the blood of Jesus. Righteousness is a gift. You are a righteous new creature.

FIRST CLASS RIGHTEOUSNESS

I do a lot of international flying and know that you can fly tourist class, business class, or first class. I have had the blessing of flying first class on occasion and have noticed there is a great deal of difference between the service in first class and tourist class.

When you come on the plane in first class, immediately the attendant will make sure you have everything to make you comfortable. You are offered something to drink or eat. They will take your coat, make sure you have a blanket or pillow, and help you put up your belongings.

However, in tourist class they almost act irritated that you are there! And don't ask them for anything special. They'll tell you to get it yourself. The seating isn't so comfortable.

If you have an aisle seat, you can look up the aisle and see into first class, and you know things are much better up there. But you are stuck in tourist class! After awhile they won't even let you look. They pull a curtain as if to say you don't even deserve to look into first class! You develop a real tourist mentality as the person next to you goes to sleep and snores and slobbers. However, God spoke to me through all of this and said, "There is no *Tourist-Class Righteousness*. All of the God-kind of righteousness is *First-Class Righteousness!*"

The moment anyone receives Jesus, that man or woman is made the righteousness of God. You are heirs of God and joint-heirs with Christ. You reign as kings in life because of God's grace and the gift of righteousness. When You come on board *in Christ*, all heaven stands at attention. The blessings of heaven are yours in Him. The authority of heaven is yours in His Name. God is your very own Father, and you are His very own children.

The blessings and benefits of righteousness are listed throughout the Old and New Testaments. In Him you have been made the righteousness of God. Understanding righteousness has a mighty effect on every area of your life, including your prayer life. James 5:16 says, *The earnest (heartfelt, continued) prayer of a righteous man makes tremendous power available, [dynamic in its working],* (The Amplified Bible).

Smith Wigglesworth said, "You need to see how wonderful you are in God and how helpless you are in yourself." You must see yourself *in Christ*, Without Him, you could do nothing. Jesus said, *If ye abide in me, and my words abide in you, ye shall ask what ye will, and it shall be done unto you* (John 15:7). You have tremendous power in prayer when you abide *in Christ* and His words abide in you.

FREEDOM FROM GUILT AND SIN CONSCIOUSNESS

God does not want His children to live with a continual consciousness of sin, failure, defeat, weakness, guilt, and inferiority.

As a father of two children, I know I don't want my children to live that way.

God is your heavenly Father, and He is glorified when you reflect His life, joy, and victory. This does not mean that you won't have challenges. You live in a world that is full of adversity, but you are overcomers, because you are born of God, (I John 5:4). Instead of a sense of sin or guilt, you should have a sense of righteousness and triumph.

The apostle Paul said, *Now thanks be unto God, which always causeth us to triumph in Christ, and maketh manifest the savour of his knowledge by us in every place* (II Cor.2:14). *In Christ* is your place of triumph. Notice Paul said, in every place. The savour is the smell of victory. Paul was in some difficult places, but he said, I keep smelling like the victory of Jesus. Paul was shipwrecked, snakebit, beaten in the head, and left for dead, yet he came out saying, I am more than a conqueror *in Christ*. He came out smelling like a rose with victory over the world, the flesh, and the devil. Paul saw himself *in Christ*.

Some people have been through some very tough things, and they came out smelling like their bad experience. God wants you to keep smelling like the triumph of Christ. This means you have to live in the consciousness and with the confession of who you are *in Christ*.

THE SMELL OF TRIUMPH

Several years ago on one of our family vacations, I decided to drive through a wild animal park in Oklahoma. We purchased some small buckets of feed to give to the various animals as we drove through.

My daughter, Alicia, was sitting in the front passenger seat, and my wife, Trina, and my son, Aaron, were sitting in the back seat.

At first, all we saw were deer, so we fed the deer and they were nice and cute. However, about that time a llama came strolling up on Alicia's side of the van, and he scared her so much that, she quickly pushed the power switch and her window went up.

I laughed and said, "I'm not afraid of a llama." He must have heard me say that because immediately he came to my side of the van. I began to feed him out of my bucket, and he finally forced his whole head in the window and was eating out of my bucket with his whole head in my lap. Alicia and I began to laugh nervously, and the llama pulled his head out of the bucket and sneezed in my van. Llama spit and snot and slimy stuff went all across the front dash and on our clothes. It was nasty and had a terrible smell. I immediately slapped the llamas head to get him out and rolled up the window, but the damage had been done.

We left the park and headed for the nearest store to get something to clean up the mess. We finally got the slime out, but the smell was more difficult. During our whole vacation, each morning as we would get in the van, we could smell the llama sneeze. That smell stayed in there for months before we finally got it out. The llama was gone, but the smell was still there!

That's the way sin and Satan are. When the devil gets his head in your life, he will not leave until he has sneezed and made a mess. But the reason Jesus shed His blood, died, and rose from the dead for you was to undo all that the devil had done. God not only wants to get the devil's head out and clean up the mess, He wants you to be free from the smell of the past. God doesn't want you to smell like sin, failure, guilt, and shame.

He wants you to apply the blood of Jesus to your life in every situation and smell like the triumph of Christ. *In Christ* you have a sense of righteousness and victory. You can forget about the past and press on for the high calling of God today and the future. If you have sinned, I John 1:7 says, *"But if we walk in the light, as he is in the light, we have fellowship one with another, and the blood of Jesus Christ his Son cleanseth us from all sin."* Verse 9 says, *If we confess our sins, he is faithful and just to forgive us our sins, and to cleanse us from all unrighteousness.* Thank God for the blood of Jesus and your place in *Christ* Jesus! Ephesians 3:12 says, *In whom we have boldness and access with confidence by the faith of him.*

YOUR IDENTIFICATION WITH CHRIST

Paul said:

I have been crucified with Christ and I no longer live, but Christ lives in me. The life I live in the body, I live by faith in the Son of God, who loved me and gave himself for me.

Galatians 2:20 (New International Version)

In this verse, the substitutionary work of Christ and His love for you is revealed. Paul's understanding of Christianity is based on *substitution* — what Christ has done for you — and on *identification* that Jesus took your place and died your death so that you might live. Everything Jesus did, He did for you. It is set to the credit of your account as though you did it. Jesus gave Himself for you. He died in your place. Now you can see how God changes your identity!

AN IDENTITY CHANGE

Paul is not talking about a spiritual state that he has come to. Rather, he is talking about what happened on the cross in the death, burial, and resurrection of Christ, and what happened the moment he accepted Jesus as his Lord and Savior. *Paul is talking about an identity change.*

This means the moment you say "yes" to Jesus, not some thirty years later — you can say, "I was crucified with Christ: nevertheless I live; yet not I, but Christ lives in me." (Galatians 2:20)

"I have been crucified with Christ." (NEB, NIV, NASV, RSV, Gspd, ASV, Moff, Weym, AMP, Wms, NBerk, Pl Eng, Barclay)

The Noli Translation says, *I have been crucified with Christ. Now it is not my old self, but Christ himself who lives in me.*

To be crucified with Christ means the old self, the old person you used to be, is gone and now Christ Himself lives in you. You ought to be doing very well if Christ Himself is living in you! He has conquered the devil, the world, and the flesh. He is triumphant.

You can get real mental about this and say, "I wonder what he is trying to say?" If you think too much about it, you will never figure it out. Accept it at face value and declare, "This is God's revelation of Christianity. It is who I am and what I have. I have been crucified with Christ. Christ Himself now lives in me." Hallelujah!

The Cressman Translation says, *I died when Christ died on the cross. I do not live now, but Christ lives in me."*

The Jerusalem Translation of Galatians 2:20 reads:

I have been crucified with Christ, and I live now not with my own life but with the life of Christ who lives in me. The life I now live in this body I live in faith: faith in the Son of God who loved me and who sacrificed himself for my sake.

Recently, after I taught a class about identification with Christ, one person said to me, "Pastor, all the sermons I have ever heard about what happened on the cross always identified us with the crowd, like the Roman soldiers, Mary the mother of Jesus, the disciples, or someone in the crowd who was hollering, `Crucify Him.' No one ever told us, that Jesus identified with us and we are identified with Him."

Laubach's Translation of Galatians 2:20 is my favorite. It says, *Christ took me to the cross with Him, and I died there with Him.* That means you were crucified together with Him when He was crucified. This is the most powerful aspect of your Redemption. If you died with Him, Paul says, "we were, made alive, raised, and seated with Him" (Ephesians 2:4-6).

WERE YOU THERE?

The old Gospel hymn says, "Were you there when they crucified my Lord...Were you there when he was buried Were you there when he was raised up from the grave...Sometimes it causes me to tremble...."

I remember hearing that song as a child and thinking, Of course, "I wasn't there. That happened 2,000 years ago." I did not understand Paul's revelation. I did not understand what happened "in the Spirit" or what God saw happening in the death, burial, and resurrection of Christ.

The Holy Spirit through the apostle Paul says, "We were there in the death, burial, resurrection, triumph, and seating of Jesus Christ."

More happened on the cross and in the resurrection than can be seen with the natural eye. The Gospel is a group picture. Jesus took you with Him. That is the X ray picture. That is what God saw. When you see what God saw, it will make you tremble sometimes. The power and the glory of God are yours *in Christ*.

THE GOSPEL IS A GROUP PICTURE

Since the Gospel is a group picture, the first thing you look for in a group picture is yourself. By faith you find yourself in the death, burial, and resurrection of Christ. You don't look too good on the cross, but in the resurrection you look great in Him.

WHAT HAPPENED AT THE CROSS

Sometimes even theologians and historians struggle with Scripture that talks about our *identity* with Christ. They say, "The apostle Paul is kind of a loony tune, you know, because he says he was crucified with Christ. We know Paul was not crucified with Christ, because he was not even in Jerusalem when Jesus was crucified. So how could he have been crucified with Christ? Jesus was on the center cross. There was a thief on one side and a criminal on the other, so how could Paul say he was crucified with Christ?"

I believe Paul was talking about revelation knowledge of what happened in the Spirit when Jesus was crucified, buried, and resurrected.

You can approach what happened on the cross with a sentimental view; however, it will not cause a change in your identity. For example, people may cry or get goosebumps while watching a drama of the cross and the resurrection of Christ. But give them about three days, and they will be back in the bar. When there is no change in their identity, they will go right back into sin.

If you really want to strike at the root of your old sinful nature and have an identity change, there must be revelation knowledge of what happened in the death, burial and resurrection of Christ — not just a sentimental or ceremonial view. People can believe an innocent man died, but that's not the real view of the cross. Jesus was innocent. He knew no sin, and He was made to be sin for us. It was not the Roman soldiers who crucified Him, because Jesus said:

...I lay down my life, that I might take it again.

No man taketh it from me, but I lay it down of myself.

John 10:17,18

JESUS TOOK US WITH HIM

You may be asking, "What took Jesus to the cross, then?" It wasn't the Roman soldiers. It wasn't even the Jews. What really took Christ to the cross was *the need for Him to take you and me with Him.* In other words, it was planned ahead of time, and Jesus was made to be sin for us. He took our sin. We died there with Him!

Don't get mad at any group of people for Jesus' crucifixion. Instead, get mad at sin and the devil, and recognize what God did for you in Jesus' death, burial, and resurrection.

Ephesian 4:17

Eph 1-117-
Change me
Have a frins

SENSE KNOWLEDGE OR REVELATION KNOWLEDGE?

There are two kinds of knowledge: sense knowledge and revelation knowledge. *Sense knowledge* refers to what you learn through your five senses, while *revelation knowledge* comes from the Word of God by the Holy Spirit.

REVELATION KNOWLEDGE

An example of revelation knowledge is found in Matthew 16, when Jesus asked His disciples, *Whom do men say that I the Son of man am?* (v. 13). The disciples responded, *Some say that thou art John the Baptist: some, Elias; and others, Jeremias, or one of the prophets* (v. 14). Then Jesus asked, *But whom say ye that I am?* (v. 15).

Simon Peter, through revelation knowledge, spoke up, *Thou art the Christ, the Son of the living God* (v. 16).

Jesus said to Simon Peter, *Flesh and blood hath not revealed it unto thee, but my Father which is in heaven* (v. 17). In other words, "You didn't learn this through your five senses. You learned it through revelation knowledge."

This is why Paul prayed in Ephesians 1 that God *would give unto you the spirit of wisdom and revelation in the knowledge of him* (v. 17). Paul wasn't referring to just learning more about God.

REVEALED BY THE HOLY SPIRIT

Revelation knowledge comes when the eyes of your spirit are opened up. It is when the Holy Spirit transmits the things of Christ. God is a Spirit, and His truths are revealed through your spirit. You see something that no one else in the natural realm sees. You see that God has done something that is not natural perse.

When Jesus was crucified, Paul was nowhere near, yet he said, *Christ took me to the cross with Him, and I died there with Him.* (Galatians 2:20 Laubach). Where did he get that information? Paul must have gotten it from God Himself. When did he get that information? He must have gotten it when he was out in the wilderness of Arabia during those years when Jesus came and revealed to him what happened in His death and resurrection. That was *revelation knowledge* or knowledge revealed by the Holy Spirit.

When Jesus died on the cross, He took every man unto Himself. He died our death.

If you go by head knowledge (your senses or mental assent), the Word of God will lose its effectiveness and its power.

NEW UNDERSTANDING

Revelation knowledge opens the Word up to you. In the case of Galatians 2:20, through revelation knowledge you understand, "I have a new identity. It is no longer I who live, but Christ lives in me."

Do you think Paul was crucified with Christ? He said he was. He is not saying it exclusively as the apostle Paul, but he is talking about what happened in the death and resurrection of Christ as your Substitute. Jesus became your Substitute, so everything He did, He did to the credit of your account.

Arthur S. Way says, "Yes, I have shared Messiah's crucifixion. I am living indeed, but it is not I that live; it is Messiah whose life is in me." The Distilled Bible says, "I consider myself as having died and now enjoying a second existence, which is simply Jesus using my body."

THE CENTER OF THE GOSPEL

It is important to understand your identification with Christ in His crucifixion and resurrection, because it is at the center of the Gospel. You won't hear a sermon on this in many churches even if you stay there for ten years. They are trying so hard to deal with everybody's personal problems — keeping people from having nervous breakdowns, teaching them how to love their wife or husband, and how to discipline their kids, how to get their healing, and how to get their needs met.

The level of the manifestation of Christ in you is based on *revelation knowledge* of the Word and mixing faith with it. It is also based upon your yieldedness to the Holy Spirit, because the Holy Spirit is the One Who reveals Christ. That is His job. The greater your Word intake, the more Christ will be manifested through you.

YOUR IDENTITY WITH CHRIST

Every day you can declare, "I was crucified with Christ. It is not my old self who lives, but Christ Himself lives in me. The life I live in this body, I live by faith in the Son of God who loved me and gave Himself for me."

If you preach on your identity with Christ in many churches, people will look at you like a cow at a new gate or a dog at a new pan. They will say, "You don't understand. I'm trying to make my refrigerator payment, I've got pain in my lower back, and I'm having trouble with my kids. I need new carpet in my house, I'm dealing with emotional problems and stress, and you are talking about *identification with Christ*. That's not what I need." Yet an understanding of their identity *in Christ* is exactly what they need!

HOW GOD CHANGES PEOPLE'S IDENTITIES

Paul had such a radical identity change, he said, "It's not even me living anymore." That's a pretty violent change! People are trying to get God to help them deal with their problems. Yet He is saying, "As my child, since I am living on the inside of you, just let Me deal with your challenges through you."

A WHOLE NEW IDENTITY

Someone said, "The power of God hit Saul of Tarsus so hard on the road to Damascus that it knocked the "S" off the front of his name, replaced it with a "P" and he became Paul." His name changed, his identity changed, and his nature changed. Paul was a Pharisee, a very religious man, and he received a strong revelation of Jesus Christ. When he was hit with the light of God, he went blind for three days. During that time, he fasted and prayed.

I believe the moment you receive Christ, you become a new creation in Him, but it takes a while to feed on the Word before you say, "I'm not even the same person anymore. I have a whole new identity."

If you committed a crime and the CIA got hold of you and

wanted to give you a new identity to protect you, they would change your address, your Social Security number and all records concerning every bill that you owe. They would totally wipe out your past to protect you.

God wiped out your old identity when you were born again. He wiped out your past. Every account, sin, or claim the devil had on you has been wiped out. Once you are lost *in Christ*, the devil can't even find you! Hallelujah!

Colossians 3:3 says, *For ye are dead, and your life is hid with Christ in God.* The devil can't even find you unless you stick your fleshly head up and say, "Hey, it's me!" Slap your head and get it back down in there, man!

You want to talk about my past? My feelings? My failures? God says, "I don't want to talk about that. You are dead and your life is hid with Christ in Me. Don't stick your head up. You've got a new identity now."

A NEW LIFE IN CHRIST

God made provision for you to be *in Christ*, even before you were saved, but this new identity didn't become yours until you exercised faith in Him when you were born again. You became a new creation *in Christ* the day you were saved. But it won't become a reality to you unless you walk in the light of the Word. You'll have to feed on the Word, get it engrafted on the inside of you and receive revelation knowledge of the Word. Then let the Holy Spirit help you to see your new identity — who you are *in Christ* and what you have in Him.

Second Corinthians 5:17 in The Twentieth Century New Testament says:

So, if any one is in union with Christ, he is a new being! His old life has passed away, and a new life has begun!

FROM CHILDLESS TO FATHER OF MANY

One of the greatest stories ever written in the greatest Book ever written (the Bible) on changing one's identity is the story of God appearing to Abram and Sarai. God basically said, "I'm changing your identity, and I'm changing your name. You will never be called Abram again. You are *Abraham*, which means 'father of many'. And Sarai, I'm changing your name to *Sarah*, which means `you are a princess.'" (Genesis 17).

I believe every time Sarah and Abraham called each other, they declared what God said they were. Yet "Abraham, father of many," didn't have any children at that point in his life. That's how God does business. If He can get you to agree with Him to agree with revelation knowledge — His Word will not return unto Him void. It will accomplish what He sent it out to do, and it will prosper in the thing whereto He sent it (Isaiah 55:11). In other words, the Word has the power to produce what it says if God can get you to agree with it.

Abraham became the father of many nations as well as the father of your faith. God totally changed his identity. You wouldn't recognize him years later as the man who left Ur of the Chaldees at God's direction.

FROM COUNTRY BOY TO PROPHET

God is in the business of changing identities. One of my favorite stories of how God totally changed someone's identity is with Saul in 1 Samuel chapters 9 and 10. Saul was looking for his father's donkeys when he met Samuel the prophet. Samuel told him:

Go up before me unto the high place; for ye shall eat with me to day, and to morrow I will let thee go, and will tell thee all that is in thine heart.

1 Samuel 9:19

The prophet told Saul, *[You will] meet a company of prophets...And the Spirit of the Lord will come upon thee, and thou shalt prophesy with them, and shalt be turned into another man* (1 Samuel 10:5,6).

The prophet Samuel was saying, "Saul, you are a country boy, but the Holy Ghost will come on you, and you are going to be changed into another man." Saul received a totally new identity.

YOUR VALUE IN CHRIST

How did this happen? He didn't go to every self-help and support group in an attempt to get a new identity. He didn't consult a psychologist or call the psychic hotline! If that had been the case, I would have said, "Saul, you are messed up. You are messing with devils and trying everything after the flesh. You can get a whole new identity when you see who God says you are and what God says you have. Your self-esteem will go right through the roof! You will say, "Glory to God! Look what God says I am. Look at the value God has given me *in Christ.*"

The devil wants to destroy your dignity and self-esteem, but when you see your value in what God has done for you in the death and resurrection of Christ, you will hold your head up high and forget those things which are behind. You will say, "The person who did those things, acted that way, and thought that way is dead." Glory to God!

CHANGED FROM WITHIN

God can give you a new identity. He made you, so He ought to be able to remake you. He is the Manufacturer! We are not dealing with someone who just repairs. We are talking about the One Who creates people.

God creates people out of nothing! No scientist has ever figured out how to make people. Natural man can make houses, toasters and color TVs, but they aren't making people! God is a Creator. He is the original people person. He specializes in making people over again and giving them brand new identities.

In Jeremiah 18, the Spirit of God spoke through Jeremiah:

Arise, and go down to the potter's house, and there I will cause thee to hear my words.

Then I went down to the potter's house, and, behold, he wrought a work on the wheels.

And the vessel that he made of clay was marred in the hand of the potter: so he made it again another vessel, as seemed good to the potter to make it.

Jeremiah 18:2-4

God was telling Jeremiah, "You go down to the potter's house, and I am going to show you that when people have defects in them, I will make them over again."

God is in the business of changing people's identities. He does it from the inside out. When you are born again, your spirit is recreated. Then He builds from the inside out — changing your mind, renewing it, rebuilding your thinking and attitudes, then changing your body and your actions.

Philippians 2:13 says, *For it is God which worketh in you both to will and to do of his good pleasure.*

FROM COWARD TO MIGHTY MAN OF VALOUR

Another classic yet radical identity change that took place in the Bible was with Gideon. He was living in a hole in the ground and hiding out from the enemy. You live in a hole in the ground long enough, and you will develop a certain philosophy about life. If you don't think so, go find someone who lives under a bridge. You talk to them very long, and you will find out they don't just have a bridge externally; they have a bridge internally in their thinking and attitude.

When Jesus came to preach the Gospel to the poor, He didn't just pass out a bunch of fish sandwiches! He taught them the ways and thoughts of God. He taught them that they didn't have to be poor or sick or defeated anymore. Jesus is still changing people's identities!

Every time Gideon tried to do anything, the Midianites

destroyed it. In the midst of his hole-in-the-ground existence, God sent an angel to Gideon with a message: *The Lord is with thee, thou mighty man of valour* (Judges 6:12). God has a sense of humor, because at this time in Gideon's life, there is absolutely no evidence of valor!

Yet His Word is all that you need. Scripture says *He ...quickeneth the dead, and calleth those things which be not as though they were* (Romans 4:17). God's Word will cause "nothing" to become "something."

Gideon chewed on God's Word to him — "you mighty man of valour" — until he finally swallowed it. Then with a cry of "the sword of the Lord" (Judges 7:20), trumpets, pitchers, and lamps, Gideon and his three hundred-man army whipped the enemy.

Any time you get involved with God and His Word, He will totally change the way you see yourself and the way you see life. *The Word of God changes everything.*

MY NAME IS ROCK

As I mentioned earlier, when Simon Peter received revelation knowledge of who Jesus was — the Christ, the Son of the living God (Matthew 16:16) — Jesus turned to him and said, "I'm telling you who you are, Simon. No longer will you be tossed to and fro. I am changing your name to 'rock'" (author's paraphrase).

Can't you just see Simon responding to the people who wouldn't accept his new name? You know, "Your mama named you Simon." "Jesus is the One Who named me, and my name is rock!" Peter totally identified with who Jesus said he was. Jesus changed his identity.

LET ME TELL YOU WHO I AM

Another identity change took place in the life of John the Baptist. When he came out of the wilderness preaching, some of the Jews asked, *Who art thou?* (John 1:19).

When John the Baptist said, *I am not the Christ* (v. 20), the Jews asked, "Art thou Elias? And he saith, I am not. Art thou that prophet? And he answered, No" (v. 21). As they continued to press him for his identity, John the Baptist said, *I am the voice of one crying in the wilderness, Make straight the way of the Lord, as said the prophet Esaias [Isaiah]* (v. 23). In other words, John the Baptist said, "Let me tell you who I am."

What would happen every time the devil comes to you and says, "Who do you think you are?" and you just open your Bible and say, "Let me tell you who I am. I have no other identity but Galatians 2:20. I was crucified with Christ. Nevertheless I live, yet not I, but Christ lives in me."

KNOW YOUR IDENTITY IN CHRIST

It is important to know who you are, because the devil knows whether you know your identity *in Christ.*

When the seven sons of Sceva tried using the Name of Jesus to cast out evil spirits without having a relationship with Jesus which would give them authority to use His Name, an evil spirit said to them, *Jesus I know, and Paul I know; but who are ye?* (Acts 19:15).

Because they didn't know their identity *in Christ,* Scripture says, *The evil spirit...leaped on them, and overcame them, and prevailed against them, so that they fled out of that house naked and wounded* (v. 16).

YOUR IDENTITY IN THE WORD

As a born-again, Spirit-filled teenager, I was struggling with my own identity. While in my bedroom studying from Luke chapter 4, where Jesus went into the synagogue to preach His first sermon, I read, *And there was delivered unto him the book of the prophet Esaias. And when he had opened the book, he found the place where it was written* (v. 17).

The Holy Ghost spoke to me, "Though Jesus was deity, He laid aside His deity power when He became a man, and in His humanity, He had to study the Word to find out who He was." I believe when Jesus was ten, eleven, or twelve years old, He found out who He was by reading it in the Scriptures.

Luke 2:52 says, *And Jesus increased in wisdom and stature, and in favour with God and man.* Jesus identified with the Word as He read Isaiah 61:1:

stop

The Spirit of the Lord God is upon me; because the Lord hath anointed me to preach good tidings unto the meek; he hath sent me to bind up the brokenhearted, to proclaim liberty to the captives, and the opening of the prison to them that are bound.

You will find your identity in the same Book, the Bible. You won't find it in some psychology book or by trying to mimic a movie star. Many people, not just teenagers, have an identity crisis. They comb their hair like someone they see on TV. They watch some cowboy movie and think they are John Wayne. Or they see a motorcycle rider and think they need a motorcycle and a bandanna around their head, too.

The devil will do everything he can to steal the Word from you to keep you from understanding your new identity *in Christ*. He wants you to see yourself in the natural. He will even get you to study your family tree — which never produced anything but a bunch of nuts! In identifying with your family, instead of with Christ, you may say, "The reason I am divorced is because my mother, grandmother, and great — grandmother were divorced. My daddy was an alcoholic, my grandpa was an alcoholic, so I'm an alcoholic. It just runs in my family."

You need to find your identity from God. He knows who you are. You are an individual created to reflect His glory. If the devil can get you to flip-flop mentally with your reasoning and your flesh, he will totally defeat you.

CHRIST LIVES IN YOU

The apostle Paul said, "I only have one identity and that is who I am *in Christ* Jesus. I don't identify with anything or anyone else. I was crucified with Christ. Nevertheless I live, yet not I, but Christ lives in me."

You can go to almost any insane asylum and find someone who thinks he is Napoleon. Often, people are controlled by familiar spirits and natural connections instead of taking the Word of God and letting God establish their identity.

Jesus *initiated* your identification with God when He became a man. In His humanity, He identified with you so He could know how you feel, what you go through, and the struggles you face. But He didn't totally identify with you until He went to the cross, where He took your sinful condition and your curse.

Then He *sealed* your identification with God on the cross, because when Jesus died on the cross, He was not a man for one human generation. He became a man forever. He is still a man right now, seated at the right hand of God, representing a new, victorious humanity.

Once you understand your identification with Christ in His death, burial, and resurrection, it will take you from His death, burial, and resurrection right through to triumph, where Christ is seated at the right hand of God. Never again will you identify with defeat, failure, depression, fear, sickness, poverty, or lack once your identification with Christ is sealed. Why? Because it is no longer you who live, but Christ lives in you!

That means no longer are you going under, but you are going over. I was under when I had no identification with Christ. But God stamped in my spirit the death, burial, and resurrection of Christ.

Some people may never know their earthly father. However, they don't have to spend their entire life with a big gap in their souls. They can just say, "I am identified with Christ, and God is my Father."

You are a totally different person than when you were born. Even if your daddy or mama was a failure, when you are born again, you are re-fathered! If you come from a dysfunctional family, when you are born again, you receive a functional family — the family of God. That's your identification with Christ.

Don't you ever let the devil bring up your past, show you pictures of it, and say, "That's who you are." You tell him, "You are a lying dog. Get out of my life. That old person is dead and gone. I am crucified with Christ. Nevertheless I live, yet Christ Himself lives in me."

CONFESS YOUR IDENTITY IN CHRIST

Begin to confess what God's Word says about your identification with Christ. Here are a few sample confessions:

In Christ Jesus, the world is crucified unto me and I unto the world (Galatians 6:14.).

Since I am risen with Christ, I seek those things which are above. My affection is set on things above, not on things on the earth. My life is hid with Christ in God (Colossians 3:1-3).

I am buried with Christ by baptism into death. Just as Christ was raised up from the dead by the glory of the Father, even so I walk in newness of life (Romans 6:4).

My old sin nature is crucified with Christ. I no longer serve sin (Romans 6:6).

God, who is rich in mercy and love for me, has quickened me together with Christ, raised me up, and made me sit together in heavenly places in Christ Jesus (Ephesians 2:4-6).

Now that we have established a foundation of who you are *in Christ*, in the next chapter we will look at the inheritance He left for you, which is yours *now!*

YOUR INHERITANCE IN CHRIST

Therefore if any man be in Christ, he is a new creature [or creation]: old things are passed away; behold, all things are become new.

And all things are of God, who hath reconciled us to himself by Jesus Christ, and hath given to us the ministry of reconciliation.

2 Corinthians 5:17,18

In verse 18, when Paul says, *And all things are of God,* he is not just saying that everything is of God. He is literally talking about all of these things of the new creation. Other translations say, "This is the work of God."

The apostle Paul is talking about *who you are in Christ Jesus.* He is talking about the miracle of the New Birth — what happens when you are born again.

IN CHRIST-ED

Several Scriptures use this phrase *in Christ.* It really helped me when I was seventeen years old to look up all the *in Christ* Scriptures — all 130 of them.

When you are born again, I like to say, "You are *in Christed!*" As a believer in Jesus Christ, you are *in Christ,* and whatever is true of someone *in Christ* is true of you. As I went through the *in*

Christ Scriptures as a teenager, I would get my guitar and sing and pray them over and over. I would declare, "I am who God says I am, and I have what God says I have. I can do what God says I can do."

I did that for hours. I'm not talking about just during a youth revival or campmeeting; I'm talking about day after day. I sang and prayed the Ephesians prayers everyday. If you will pray these prayers every day, I guarantee your life will be different in six months' time.

If you are happy with your life the way it is, just keep doing what you are doing, and it will stay that way or even get worse. But if you want things to change for the better, I challenge you to pray the Ephesians prayers every day. Pray them over your children, even if they are grown and married. Pray them over your husband or wife.

In the Ephesians 1 prayer, Paul prayed that God would give you a spirit of wisdom and revelation in the knowledge of Him; that the eyes of your understanding would be enlightened; that you would know the hope of His calling; the riches of His inheritance in the saints; the exceeding greatness of His power to us who believe, according to the working of His mighty power, which He wrought *in Christ* when He raised Him from the dead (v. 17-20).

In God's economy, something happened when He raised Christ from the dead:

Righteousness was restored to man.

The devil was defeated.

The curse was broken.

Man was restored to fellowship with God.

Redemption was accomplished.

These provisions became yours when you said, "Yes, Jesus, I surrender to You. I want You to be Lord of my life." Once you said "yes" to Jesus, you were "*in Christed*"! All that God did *in Christ* became personally yours.

To be *in Christ* means that you have been blessed with all spiritual blessings in heavenly places *in Christ* (Ephesians 1:3). As a teenager, I would sing this Scripture. I would also sing Ephesians 2:10, "I am God's workmanship, created *in Christ* Jesus for good works, which God ordained that I should walk in."

God doesn't make any trash, you know. If you are the workmanship of God, you must be something wonderful!

GOD HAS PREPARED THE WAY

God has prepared a path ahead of time for His children to walk. When you walk in that path, everything you need is found on it.

When you are born again, the moment you confess Jesus Christ as your Lord and Savior, your spirit receives eternal life. Romans 10:13 says, *For whosoever shall call upon the name of the Lord shall be saved.* Did you know that you can get saved in your car, working in your backyard, or walking down the aisle in the grocery store? Even a person who cries out to Jesus with his or her last breath of life is born again.

When you are born again, you pass from death to life. We are referring to spiritual death. Paul said, *And you hath he quickened, who were dead in trespasses and sins* (Ephesians 2:1).

Before you received Jesus, you weren't *physically* or *mentally* dead, but you were *spiritually* dead, which means you were alienated or separated from God. Because you were spiritually dead, Satan was able to exercise dominion over you.

FREED FROM SATAN'S DOMINION

The moment you were born again, your spirit received eternal life. You left Satan's dominion and entered the dominion of the Lord Jesus Christ. Legally, Satan no longer has any control over you. In fact, he cannot touch you. You are *in Christ*. You are *in* this world, but you are not of it. Satan will still try to come against you, but you have left his jurisdiction. Colossians 1:13 says:

Who hath delivered us from the power of darkness, and hath translated us into the kingdom of His dear Son: Rotherham's translation says, "...the authority of the darkness." To explain leaving Satan's authority or jurisdiction, think of a policeman assigned to Alexandria, Louisiana. He has no jurisdiction, in Texas, so he can't give you a ticket in Texas. He has no authority there.

The moment you pass from death to life, you leave Satan's jurisdiction, and you enter into the jurisdiction of the Lord Jesus Christ. So you can say, "Mr. Devil, you have no dominion over me. Sickness, poverty, and sin, you have no dominion over me, because I left death and have entered life."

John 5:24 says:

Verily, verily, I say unto you, He that heareth my word, and believeth on Him that sent me, hath everlasting life, and shall not come into condemnation; but is passed from death unto life.

Jordan's translations says, "...has spiritual life...has transferred from the death region to the life region."

There are 130 things that are true about you right now. You are the righteousness of God *in Christ*. You are always triumphant *in Christ*. Victory is yours. Christ has redeemed you. Redemption is yours *in Christ*. If the devil cannot stop you from getting saved, after you are saved, he wants to cheat you out of your inheritance and keep you ignorant of what belongs to you *in Christ*.

Colossians 2:9,10 says:

For in him dwelleth all the fulness of the Godhead bodily.

And ye are complete in him, which is the head of all principality and power.

That simply means the moment you are born again, you get "*in Christed,*" and whatever is *in Christ* is now in you.

JOINED TO CHRIST

First Corinthians 6:17 says, *But he that is joined unto the Lord is one spirit.* When you are born again, your spirit is joined to Jesus. Weymouth's translation says, *But he that is in union with the Master is one with Him in spirit.* The Living Bible says, *But if you give yourself to the Lord, you and Christ are joined together as one person.*

If the only purpose for salvation was for you to go to heaven, God would have built in a special death mechanism that as soon as you confess Jesus as Lord, you would die right then. Actually, God saved you so heaven could get on the inside of you, and then *you could change the world around you.*

God saved you to conform to the image of His Son so you could be all God has created and designed you to be. There is more to life than thirty years of mortgage payments, polyester suits, Toyotas, Cadillacs, and Mercedes! When you are saved, you are put in union with Christ so the same life, glory, joy, authority, power, inheritance, future, blessings — the same stuff that is *in Christ* comes in you!

God saved you so that you could *bring heaven into this earth and change the world.* God saved you to change your children, your neighborhood, and your city. God saved you so He could move on the inside of you. He saved you so your mind would work right. He saved you so you wouldn't be a victim of sin, bad habits, lust, and deception. He freed you from Satan's dominion so when you die, you won't wonder why you lived. God saved you for Christ to be formed in you! Instead of sitting around with a sanctimonious look on your face like you've been sucking oats through a gas pipe, what would happen if you found out what *really* took place when you were saved?

DELIVERED FROM SIN

The word *saved means daily delivered from sin's dominion* (Romans 5:10 Amplified). It means delivered not only from sin that grips and controls people's lives, but from the effects of sin that shuts down the glory of God and your production as a child of God. When sin takes hold of you, you are absolutely worthless to the Kingdom of God. Your confidence goes, the gift of God in you gets messed up, and you sit around in deception, shame, and guilt, trying to smile and act like everything is all right.

When you were saved, Jesus moved on the inside of you so He could invade your mind, your soul, your emotions, your intellect and your body. He filled you up with His life so it can flow out of you into your husband or wife and your children.

The apostle Paul said, "I am a new creation *in Christ*." Dead religion could not do that for Paul. He was a Pharisee. He had studied and knew the Scriptures, yet he said, "Nothing could do for me what happened on the road to Damascus when I met Jesus."

The moment you become a new creation, you need to say, "Jesus, I want to know You and I want to know what You want me to do." He will tell you both. He will say, "I am the Alpha, the Omega, the beginning and the end; the King of kings and the Lord of lords." The list could go on and on of who Jesus is. Then He will say, "Everything I have is yours!"

A SPIRITUAL CONNECTION

Some translators refer to the *in Christ* phrase as "in union with Christ." When your spirit is joined to Christ, that means the unseen part of you on the inside is connected to Christ. You say, "How could that be?"

It's not like the telephone lines where you have a very long line that goes from your spirit through the roof up into the heavens. Obviously, airplanes would get tangled up in it!

If a network is broadcasting out of New York City, you can tune in with a TV set and a receiver and receive the exact program at the same time — even if you are living in the woods some 2,000 miles away, wearing your boots, driving your four-wheeler, and piping in sunshine. There is an *unseen connection* between your TV set and what is going on in New York City.

The moment you are born again, God gives your spirit a receiver and He tunes it in to heaven, so the same thing that is playing in heaven booms on the inside of you!

Though you used to be cursed and bound, confused and messed up, you can tune in on a new picture! You are in union with Christ. Now you can see a picture of *all* that God wants you to be, a picture of the redeeming power of Jesus Christ, a picture of what God has planned for you to be. Hallelujah!

TO BE LIKE JESUS

When God made you a new creation *in Christ*, He didn't make you to be defeated, confused, sick, poor, beat up, and living on barely-get-along street. He made you to be a conqueror!

Some people say, "Brother, you preach all that healing and prosperity stuff, and it just makes me sick, because I don't need it. I just want to be like Jesus." Well, that's honorable of you. Did you know that Jesus isn't sick? He isn't poor, either.

Do you think He is sitting on the throne, saying, "Oh, my stomach is hurting. I don't know how I'm going to make it. I've got some payments coming up at the end of this month. I've been talking to the Father about them, but I don't know if I'm going to make it. I am so tired!"

That's not the way Jesus is. He is seated at the right hand of God, and the Bible says His enemies are way beneath His feet. All power in heaven and in earth has been given to Him. Everything the Father has is His. He is not sitting up there barely getting along. Instead, He is saying, *"I am he that liveth, and was dead; and, behold, I am alive for evermore, Amen; and have the keys of hell and of death"* (Revelation 1:18).

He is saying to every born-again believer, "I've got all power in heaven and earth. If you need it, you can get it from Me. If I don't have it in stock, I will *make* it just for you!"

MORE LIKE JESUS

You can be more like Jesus. He healed the sick and cast out devils. When Jesus came into a town, things changed. The devil is faithful to come back and visit. He will come back and say, "If you are really saved..." Some people have never decided if they are saved or not. From the preaching they are hearing, it is probably a wonder they have even hung around! The preacher says, "I know you did everything the Book says, but you can't ever tell." What do you mean, "You can't ever tell"? If God said it and you did it, you are saved. You can say, "You can't ever tell" all the way to your funeral. You can keep all the rules, quit wearing earrings, get all the makeup off your face, get baptized three different ways, speak in tongues, shake all over, and still not know if you are saved.

Being *in Christ* has nothing to do with your *feelings*. It has everything to do with the Word of God and the integrity of God's Word. It has everything to do with what Jesus did for you 2,000 years ago. You can get up every morning and say, "I am a new creation *in Christ* Jesus. Old things are passed away, and everything has become new."

Some people are still talking about what happened to them

when they were ten years old. There is not a thing in the world a psychologist or anyone else can do for you if something messed your life up when you were ten. But Jesus can do something. In Him you can become brand new. Old things are passed away. There is a department of your being — your spirit where at the moment you are born again, old things are passed away and everything becomes new.

There is not one little molecule left of what you used to be — not a trace! You can get all the specialists you want to try to find a trace of what you used to be, but they won't find it. They can never dig it up. It is gone forever. God will never speak of it, because it doesn't exist anymore. That's good news, and it will set you free.

10

THE UNSEEN CONNECTION

You have a partner to walk out your new life *in Christ*. His name is the Holy Spirit, or the Holy Ghost. Jesus describes the work of the Holy Ghost in John 16:13: *Howbeit when he, the Spirit of truth, is come....*

THE SPIRIT OF TRUTH

First, the Holy Spirit is a *Spirit of truth*. If you would listen to Him, He would keep you out of a lot of trouble — trouble in business, in relationships, and in church. If the preacher isn't telling you the truth, the Holy Spirit will say, "That isn't true." But if you have the Holy Ghost on the inside of you and the preacher is telling the truth, He will say, "That is the truth."

You may be thinking, "Truth doesn't excite me." What does? The casinos? Do you like all the lights and the truth that is spoken there? They will call you everything you want to be called. "Mr. Wonderful, you might be a millionaire tonight." But remember, they didn't build that place with winners! They are even glad when you win, because you will stick around and lose another $5,000. Then you will go to church and not even pay your tithes. You need a slap on the head!

What does the Holy Spirit, the Spirit of truth, do? "...he will guide into all truth." As you read your Bible, you need to invite your Holy Spirit partner, "Holy Spirit, let's read the Bible. Help me and guide me into all truth. Show me something, Holy Spirit." Since the Holy Spirit wrote it, He ought to know what it means!

YOUR HELPER

The Holy Spirit will keep you from just reading the Word with your head. He wants to show you the Bible in the light of Redemption. He will show you the weightier matters and things that are of first importance. The Holy Spirit will help you read your Bible. He will show you the things that are the most important. He won't take something out of context and mess your head up with it. That's the devil's role. The devil can quote the Bible and get you all messed up. But the Holy Spirit will show you the whole picture. He will show you who you are and what you have *in Christ.*

Smith Wigglesworth said, "The Holy Spirit never brings condemnation. He always reveals the blood of Jesus. He always lifts and helps." He tells you the truth to help you, because if you keep going the way you are going, you will get messed up!

Thank God for the Holy Ghost! Have you ever heard someone say, "I don't need to listen to the Holy Ghost." My wife is my Holy Ghost? Your wife isn't your Holy Ghost, and neither is your husband. Every person can have a relationship with the Holy Spirit. The moment you are born again, you pass from death to life, and the Spirit of God comes on the inside of you. Your body becomes the temple of the Holy Spirit.

REVEALS THINGS TO COME

...For he shall not speak of himself; but whatsoever he shall hear, that shall he speak... (John 16:13). What does it mean, "Whatsoever he shall hear, that shall he speak"? Who does the

Holy Spirit hang out with? He hangs out with the Father and the Son, so whatever He hears them say is what He says.

Verse 13 concludes, *...and he will shew you things to come.* If you want to know what is happening, you don't have to call the psychic network and ask, "What do you see in my future?" I see you going broke if you stay on that line very long! Four dollars a minute, yet you come to church and put in a dollar. You need another slap! Four dollars a minute talking to a lying devil. If it's not a devil, it's a fool who looks under cards. The cards are arranged according to states. In Louisiana, for example, they put hunting and fishing on the card. When someone from Louisiana calls, they say, "I see squirrel hunting in your future. I see a swamp in your future. I see an alligator in your future. I see crawdads in your future." That's ridiculous!

If you hang out with the Holy Ghost, and you become sensitive to Him, He will show you things to come about your life, your future, your children, your marriage, and your business. He will show you things to come about where you are going to live in the future. But He can't talk to you if you don't listen.

Be still and get with Him. Talk to Him. Worship God and worship Jesus, and then say, "Holy Spirit, help me read the Word. Show me things to come. I don't want to miss the will of God for my life. Help me."

The Holy Spirit showed me the house we are living in right now a year before we moved into it. As soon as Trina and I saw it, I said, "That's our house. I don't know how much it costs, but I know it's ours."

Before Aaron was born, I got up in the church where I was youth pastor and said, "My first child will be a boy. The Holy Ghost told me that it is a son." Then I said, "Don't bring any girl's clothes, because it's a boy."

Some people said, "We don't want you to be disappointed." I

didn't go by a sonogram, because Trina didn't have one. I went by the Holy Ghost.

One lady brought me a little dress for Aaron. I said, "My boy ain't wearing no dress! You just take it back and exchange it." She got mad and said, "You're just hardheaded, aren't you?" I said, "No, I have been praying every night for an hour and a half, and the Holy Ghost told me the baby is a boy." In the fullness of time, Aaron was born.

Two years later when Trina was pregnant again, I prayed and the Holy Ghost said, "This one is a girl." I got up in the pulpit where I was pastoring and said, "This baby is a girl. Don't bring any boy's clothes." Again, I went by the Holy Ghost, because Trina didn't have a sonogram. I had a Holy Ghost picture. He told me it was a girl. In the fullness of time, Alicia was born.

INSIDE INFORMATION

If you will spend time with the Holy Ghost, you will learn to hear His voice, and He will tell you what is going to happen a year from now, three years from now, or five years from now. He will tell you what is going to happen so you can get ready for it. The Holy Ghost can show you tragedy that is about to come in your life, in your children's lives, or in someone else's life if there isn't a change. He will show you this not to produce fear, but so you can change it in prayer. That is one of the new creation benefits. With the Holy Spirit inside of you, *you will have inside information!*

Let's read John 16:13 in its entirety:

Howbeit when he, the Spirit of truth, is come, he will guide you into all truth: for he shall not speak of himself; but whatsoever he shall hear, that shall he speak: and he will shew you things to come.

In verse 14, Jesus says:

He shall glorify me: for he shall receive of mine, and shall shew it unto you.

GLORIFIES JESUS

This means when you are full of the Holy Spirit, He will glorify Jesus. If things are happening in your life that are not bringing glory to Jesus, you can change them by praying in the Holy Ghost. He wants everyone to see what Jesus has done for them.

Jesus said, *He shall receive of mine, and shall shew it unto you.* In verse 15 Jesus said, *All things that the Father hath are mine: therefore said I, that he shall take of mine, and shall shew it unto you.*

JESUS ON THE INSIDE

The Holy Spirit is your *unseen connection* between heaven and earth, so there is a network. You are in union with Christ by virtue of the Spirit of God, so that whatever is playing in heaven is playing in your spirit. You don't have the same capacity as heaven, but you do have the same quality. You don't have the same capacity as God, but you do have the same quality of life that God has. You can enjoy a quality of life that doesn't come from, the Republicans, Democrats, welfare, or social programs!

You can enjoy a quality of life that no company can guarantee you, with no special help when you retire. You can say, "It is good, because I have the same life in me that is in God right now."

On a recent 700 Club program, Ben Kinchlow interviewed a black man who said, "I was raised in the ghetto, but the ghetto never got inside of me. There were drugs all around me, but no drugs ever got in me. Violence and crime were all around me, but they never got in me. Disaster was all around me, but it never got in me. I am here because of Jesus who got inside of me!"

Too many people let their environment shape and control

them, but this man said, *Greater is he [Jesus Christ] that is in [me], than he [the devil] that is in the world.* (1 John 4:4).

You don't have to adjust your set according to the filth, sin, lust, and violence that are all around you. You can adjust your set to heaven, where there is holiness, fire, purity, love, righteousness, and glory. I've got my set hooked up to heaven. How? I've got an unseen connection — the Holy Ghost. I am adjusting my set right now. It is tuned in. Where does all this happen? It happens in your *spirit* once you are born again.

You say, "If that is so, why am I having so many problems? It just doesn't seem real to me."

SPIRIT, SOUL, AND BODY

You are made up of three parts: spirit, soul, and body. Even after you are saved, something still has to happen in your soul — your mind, will, and emotions. Otherwise, even though you are a new creature *in Christ*, you are still acting like the world, and your spirit is held hostage to an unrenewed mind, feelings, and emotions. All kinds of trash from your past, everybody's opinions, and this world are shaping you. Your spirit is literally held hostage *until your mind is renewed with the daily washing of God's Word.*

FEED ON THE WORD

You will never be what God intends for you to be until your mind, will, and emotions are dominated by God's Word.

When you feed your spirit on the Word and allow the Holy Spirit to work in you, your mind will be renewed. The same power that is working in your spirit will move up into your head. Then God will start dealing with some of your habits and attitudes.

Initially, some people respond, "I'm not changing, I don't care what the Bible says. God understands that this is the way I am. I like a little sin on weekends and R-rated movies and pornography every now and then. I like to tell lies and dirty jokes. Sometimes I lose my temper, but that's just the way I am. I'll tithe when I want to. I'm not changing."

The Holy Spirit has a rocket missile launcher going from your spirit up to your head. It is launched as you feed upon God's Word.

John the Baptist said, "When Jesus comes, He is going to take an axe and cut the roots of that tree." If you will be still long enough in the presence of God and say, "Okay, Jesus, go ahead. I am a new creation *in Christ*. I refuse to be bound by habits, attitudes, sins, or ideas that have controlled my soul, my family and my life for ten or twenty years. I refuse to be bound. Go ahead, Jesus, let's have some changes around here," Jesus will start cleaning house then! Scripture says:

...Put off concerning the former conversation [lifestyle] the old man, which is corrupt according to deceitful lusts;

And be renewed in the spirit of your mind;

And that ye put on the new man, which after God is created in righteousness and true holiness.

Ephesians 4:22-24

BECOMING LIKE CHRIST

Even though you are born again and a new creature *in Christ*, it is a decision you must make to say, "Okay, Holy Ghost, lead me into all truth." The Holy Spirit will tell you the truth, and the truth will set you free. Why? So you can be all that God wants you to be. Wrong attitudes, compromise, sin, and disobedience will stop the flow of the life of God, so the image of Christ is not working in you and cannot be fully formed in you. You will end up dying and wonder why you ever lived.

But once you find out who you are *in Christ* and let Him be formed in you, every gift, talent, calling, and purpose of God will begin to take shape in your life.

God not only meets your needs and gives you bonuses and benefits, but as someone said, "The greatest reward for obeying God is not what you get. It's what you *become!*"

Sometimes you don't know what the true personality of a person is like because of all the trash piled on top of him or her — all the things that have happened to him or her. Let the Holy Spirit begin to work in your spirit and lead you into all truth, show you who you are *in Christ*, and you let that same picture coming from heaven play in you. You will begin to say, "I am who God says I am. I have what God says I have. I can do what God says I can do. Christ has redeemed me."

It's time for change. I'm not talking about moving to another house. I'm talking about a move on the inside of you, with your approval, "Lord, change me!"

PRAYER

Heavenly Father, I come to You now in the Name of Jesus, by the blood of Jesus, and I repent of all sin. I turn from sins of commission as well as sins of omission — things I have done that I know are wrong, attitudes that are wrong, things I knew to do but didn't do. Forgive me, Lord, and cleanse me by the blood of Jesus. I am going to follow Jesus.

I accept You now, Jesus, as my personal Lord and Savior. Now that I am saved, I am a new creation, and I am believing You for changes in my thinking and my attitudes, not by my ability, but by the Spirit of God and the Word of God working in me. Thank You that You are being formed in me, Lord Jesus. My character and my personality are being reshaped by You so I can be all You want me to be.

Lord, thank You for your mercy, for changes in my life, and for a new beginning today. I forget the past. And since You have forgiven me, I forgive myself and release the past, in Jesus' Name.

Mr. Devil, I am God's property. You have no power over my life by the blood of Jesus, by the Word of God, and by the Spirit of God. Victory is mine over the world, the flesh, and the devil — in every area of my life. Now, Father God, I am your child, and what You have started in my life You will finish. Fill me with the Holy Spirit, for I am thirsty for your plan for my life, in Jesus' Name. Amen.

11

ACKNOWLEDGING EVERY GOOD THING THAT IS IN YOU IN CHRIST

That the communication of thy faith may become effectual by the acknowledging of every good thing which is in you in Christ Jesus.

Philemon 6

When you are born again, you are *in Christ*. Someone said, "You look a whole lot better *in Christ* than you do outside of Him!" There are a lot of good things that you can acknowledge when you are *in Christ* — who you are and what you have in Him.

The Amplified Translation of Philemon 6 says, [*And I pray*] *that the participation in and sharing of your faith may produce and promote full recognition and appreciation and understanding and precise knowledge of every good* [*thing*] *that is ours in* [*our identification with*] *Christ Jesus* [*and unto His glory*].

Paul is not talking about everything that is going to be yours. He is talking about every good that that *is yours now in your identification with Christ.*

EVERY GOOD THING IN CHRIST

Often, we spend too much time focusing on our bad qualities

and what is wrong with us. If you look at what is wrong with you long enough, it will get worse. Paul is saying, "For our faith to become effective (or effectual), we need to acknowledge every good thing that is ours *in Christ.*" Your faith won't work unless you acknowledge some things. How do you *acknowledge* them? By confessing, speaking, or acting on the Word of God.

When Paul says, "Every good thing," he must mean that there is more than one good thing in you because you are *in Christ.* You can't acknowledge every good thing that is yours *in Christ* if you don't know every good thing that is yours in Him. Once you know some good things that are yours *in Christ,* your faith still won't work unless you *acknowledge* these things. Every believer needs to have a *daily* acknowledgment or confession of who he or she is and what he or she has *in Christ.*

You may question, "How long do I need to do this?" For the rest of your life! If you want your faith to work for you, you must continue to acknowledge every good thing that is yours *in Christ.*

When you first get up in the morning, when you are looking at yourself in the mirror, or before you eat breakfast, you can take time to pray and acknowledge some of the good things of who you are in *Christ.* When you are driving your truck or car, instead of doing something unprofitable or listening to some foolishness on the radio while you are sitting at a traffic light, begin to confess who you are and what you have *in Christ.* It will change your prayer life, because often you will quit asking God for things that the Word says already belong to you! The terms *in Christ, in Him,* or *in whom* refer to who you are in union with Christ. There are certain things that are yours simply because you are in union with Him.

Let's look at some of these Scripture promises. First Corinthians 1:30 says, *But of him [of God] are ye in Christ Jesus, who of God is made unto us wisdom, and righteousness, and sanctifi-*

cation, and redemption. Because you are in Christ, wisdom, righteousness, sanctification, and redemption are yours.

GOD'S WAY OF THINKING

Wisdom is God's way of thinking. God doesn't necessarily think the way you do, and He doesn't always see things the way you see them. If you want to see yourself the way God sees you, get the Word out and see what He says about you. Wisdom has to do with the revelation of all that God has done for you in the death, burial and resurrection of Christ.

To make wisdom effective in your life, you must acknowledge it. Before you go to bed at night, you need to say, "I thank God that I am in Christ Jesus, and He is made unto me wisdom. I don't have to go through life with my own thinking, my own plans, my own ways, or my own ideas. I have God's thoughts, His ways, and His plans, and His ideas. Jesus is made unto me wisdom."

RIGHTSTANDING WITH GOD

Jesus is made unto you righteousness, which is rightstanding with God. Once you are born again, you have the same standing with God that Jesus has. Hallelujah!

DEDICATION TO GOD

Jesus is made unto you righteousness. He is made unto you sanctification, which is separation from the world and dedication to God. What Jesus has begun in your life, He will bring to full completion. He is the Author and the Finisher of your faith.

DELIVERANCE AND FREEDOM

Jesus is made unto you Redemption, which means deliverance or freedom through the payment of a price. Jesus paid the price for your freedom and deliverance in every area of your life —

healing for the body, joy, freedom from oppression and depression, and freedom from poverty and the curse.

Jesus is made unto you wisdom, righteousness, sanctification, and Redemption. Every day you can say, "Jesus is made unto me wisdom, righteousness, sanctification, and Redemption. I am *in Him.*" You may be thinking, "I know all that is in the Bible, but it doesn't seem real to me." It will become real to you when you begin to *acknowledge every good thing that is yours in Christ.*

THE WORKMANSHIP OF GOD

Second Corinthians 5:17 is another good *in Christ* Scripture — *Therefore if any man be in Christ, he is a new creature: old things are passed away; behold, all things are become new.* Verse 18 begins, *And all things are of God...,* meaning, "This is the work of God." Paul is saying, "The moment you are born again, you are *in Christ,* and you are a new creature. Old things are passed away, and everything has become new."

When you are born again, you still have the same body and the same mind. You may still have some problems with your thoughts, but God says, "You are a new creation *in Christ.* Old things are passed away, and everything has become new." That is what God says about you, and that is the way He sees you.

Williams says, "...the old condition has passed away, a new condition has come." The *old condition* from which you have been redeemed is the curse of the law, which includes poverty, sickness, confusion, fear, sin, and the devil's domination of your life.

When does the "old condition" pass away and the "new condition" come? It doesn't happen over a process of ten or twenty years. It happens the moment you are born again because of the grace of God. The moment you are saved, you become a new creation *in Christ.*

I heard someone say, "God would not make an unrighteous new creature, because He already has an unrighteous old creature!" Why would He make an unrighteous new creature? This means that if you are a new creature *in Christ*, you are the righteousness of God *in Christ* (2 Corinthians 5:21).

THE REALM OF GOD

Do you think God is going to make trash? He is not going to make a confused new creature, a bound new creature, or a defeated new creature. This means the moment you are born again, He puts all of the ingredients in you that are necessary for you to be victorious in life. When we went on a cruise, we went scuba diving with the masks, special breathing equipment and flippers on our feet. Underwater we saw some of the most beautiful fish we have ever seen in our lives. It is a whole new world that you can't see from ground level. Likewise, the moment you are born again, a *whole new world opens up to you.*

In John 3:3, Jesus said, *...Except a man be born again, he cannot see the kingdom of God.* This means the minute you are born again, you can see the things you couldn't see before. You can see into the realm of God. You can see the power of God. You can see all that God has done for you *in Christ.* You move in a whole new dimension the moment you are born again!

You can scuba dive in these Scripture realities and look for a while, or you can go ahead and get one of those tanks, put it on your back, and submerge for thirty minutes or an hour.

You ask, "How in the world do you submerge?" When God's Spirit is moving and you get in God's presence, He will take you underwater and submerge you *in Christ*! He will identify you with Christ and show you who you are in Him.

This is not something you *try* to be; it is who you *are.* It is not something you try to produce. It is something God has produced for you. You are not trying to make it so. God made it so, and you can declare, "It is so."

LAUGH AT THE DEVIL

Years ago I heard about a young man who was in a Teen Challenge Program after blowing his mind on drugs. After taking a hundred hits of LSD at one time, he lost his mind. He sat on the front row in chapel day after day after day, totally out of it. One day he snapped to, stomped his foot and started laughing.

He was asked, "What happened?" He had been like a vegetable, but the Word of God is powerful. It doesn't matter what damage the devil has done in your life. If you will sit under the Word and feed on the Word, it is full of life and power.

This young man said, "Second Corinthians 5:17 hit me. As soon as it hit me, I started laughing." From that day, he walked around the Teen Challenge Center every day saying, "I am a new creature in *Christ*. Ha, ha, ha on the devil."

God restored his mind, and he went into the ministry. Without the input of God's Word, he wouldn't have amounted to anything. But the Word revealed to him who he is *in Christ*, and he started acknowledging it! He acknowledged it by daily confessing, "I am a new creature *in Christ*. Ha, ha, ha on the devil." He did that day after day after day.

People in mental institutions could have their minds restored by hearing the Word of God over and over and over again, because the Word works.

YOURS RIGHT NOW

Begin to acknowledge the Word. Begin to speak the Word. Begin to acknowledge *every good thing* that is yours *in Christ*. That means, just walk around your house saying, "I am a new creature *in Christ.* Old things are passed away. Satan's dominion over my life has passed away. Sin's dominion over my life has passed away. The curse of poverty has passed away. The curse of Satan has passed away. The curse of sickness has passed away. I'm not under the curse. I have been Redeemed. *In Christ* I have Redemption. It is mine, and I have it now."

Another Scripture that reveals who you are *in Christ* is Ephesians 1:3: *Blessed be the God and Father of our Lord Jesus Christ, who hath blessed us with all spiritual blessings in heavenly places in Christ.*

This is not something God is going to do. It is not something that is going to happen when we get to heaven. It is something that is ours *right now.* "All spiritual blessings" belong to us right now.

Norlie's says, "...who has blessed us *in Christ* with every spiritual blessing that heaven itself enjoys." In other words, whatever heaven is enjoying, the moment you are *in Christ,* you are hooked up to heaven — the joy of heaven, the peace of heaven, the victory of heaven, and the glory of heaven. You are not of this world. You have been born of God! Hallelujah!

JOINED TO CHRIST

Where does all this happen? It doesn't happen in your body, because you still have the same body. It doesn't happen in your head (in your mind), because you still have the same mind. It happens in your spirit, right down on the inside of you. *That's the real you.*

The moment you are born again, your spirit is joined to Christ. "But he that is joined unto the Lord is one spirit" (1 Corinthians 6:17). Everything the Word says about anyone *in Christ* is true about you.

COMPLETE IN CHRIST

Let's look at another good *in Christ* Scripture. Colossians 2:9,10 says: *For in him dwelleth all the fulness of the Godhead bodily.*

And ye are complete in him, which is the head of all principality and power.

Verse 10 in The Living Bible says, *So you have everything when you have Christ, and you are filled with God through your union with Christ....*

When you receive Jesus, you have everything you need for the rest of your life. You are set for the rest of your life the moment you surrender to Jesus, because He gives you wisdom, righteousness, sanctification, Redemption, and *everything* you need. The fullness of God is in Him. The riches of God's glory and His treasury are in Him. The moment you are *in Him,* you have access to the fullness of God, and you are complete in Him.

You may be thinking, "But I don't look like that." Begin to acknowledge *every good thing that is yours in Christ Jesus.*

RIGHTEOUSNESS OF GOD IN CHRIST

Second Corinthians 5:21 says, *For he hath made him to be sin for us, who knew no sin; that we might be made the righteousness of God in him.*

In most churches you wouldn't have any trouble telling people, "Jesus died on the cross for you." But they doubt the second half of that verse: "...that we might be made the righteousness of God in him." If you believe the first half of the verse, *why don't you believe the second half?*

There is a reason Jesus was made to be sin for you. Paul is talking about your righteousness *in Christ.* Being righteous means that you are accepted by God, have rightstanding with God, and are pleasing to Him. This gives you confidence in prayer and in facing the adversary, the accuser of the brethren. Paul is talking about acknowledging every good thing that is yours *in Christ*.

Romans 8:1,2 contains good *in Christ* promises:

There is therefore now no condemnation to those who are in Christ Jesus, who walk not after the flesh, but after the Spirit.

That means you have a choice whether you are going to follow the flesh or the Spirit.

For the law of the Spirit of life in Christ Jesus hath made me free from the law of sin and death.

Paul is talking about something that has already been done. Colossians 1:13,14 says:

Who hath delivered us from the power of darkness, and hath translated us into the kingdom of his dear Son:

In whom we have redemption through his blood, even the forgiveness of sins.

Our faith becomes effective as we acknowledge every good thing that is in us *in Christ* Jesus.

A SPIRITUAL DEPOSIT — NOW

If you are still believing and confessing, "I know Jesus is wonderful, but I am just a lowly little worm, and I can't do anything," you have missed the whole point. Paul is trying to tell you to acknowledge every good thing that is in you *in Christ*. He is not talking about every good thing that is *in Christ* in heaven. He is talking about in you, in the earth right now.

Jesus is no worm, and if you are in Him, you couldn't be a saved worm! The Bible says you are an heir of God and a joint-heir with Jesus Christ.

When you are born again, a spiritual deposit is made in you. We have talked about some of this deposit: *wisdom, righteousness, sanctification*, and *Redemption*.

The apostle Paul begins all his letters by stating what God has done for you *in Christ*. After he declares what God has done for you *in Christ*, he declares *who you are in Christ* and what to do about it.

TRIUMPH — ALWAYS

Another *in Christ* promise is found in 2 Corinthians 2:14: *Now thanks be unto God, which always causeth us to triumph in Christ....*

God's plan for you is to triumph *always*. Paul didn't say you would never have any tough times. I like what someone said years ago. "Tough times never last, but tough people do." Hallelujah! So how do you get to be tough? The Bible says, "...Be strong in the Lord, and in the power of his might" (Ephesians 6:10). You become strong by acknowledging who you are and what you have *in Christ*.

What do you need to do to always triumph *in Christ*? Acknowledge every good thing that is in you *in Christ*. When you get up in the morning, walk around your bedroom and say, "I give thanks unto the Father God right now that He always causes me to triumph *in Christ*. When the enemy comes against me one way, he must flee in seven ways."

God never said the enemy wouldn't try to come against you. But Isaiah 54:17 says, *No weapon that is formed against thee shall prosper....* He didn't say you wouldn't have any weapons formed against you. But he said the weapons can't prosper! In other words, when adversity comes against you, you can declare, "No weapon formed against me shall prosper." Why? Because your righteousness "...is of me, saith the Lord." The righteousness you have wasn't produced in you. It was produced by the Lord. God produced it for you *in Christ*.

RENEWING YOUR MIND

In Ephesians 4:22, Paul says:

That ye put off concerning the former conversation [He's talking about your lifestyle.] *the old man, which is corrupt according to the deceitful lusts.*

Paul is saying, "Change the way you are living." You won't change the way you are living if you don't change the way you are talking. In other words, "Quit talking the way you used to talk." The psalmist David said, *Set a watch, O Lord, before my mouth...* (Psalm 141:3). Jesus said, *For by thy words thou shalt be justified, and by thy words thou shalt be condemned* (Matthew 12:37). Proverbs 6:2 says, *Thou art snared with the words of thy mouth....*

In Ephesians 4:23,24 Paul says:

And be renewed in the spirit of your mind;

And that ye put on the new man, which after God is created in righteousness and true holiness.

Paul is discussing who we are *in Christ*. He is saying, "Here is something *you* need to do. Put off the old nature, the old lifestyle." To "put off" is like taking off the old clothes. Then he says, "Put on the new man." He gives directions how to put on the new man: *And be renewed in the spirit of your mind* (v. 23).

The process of putting off the old and putting on the new takes place as you *renew your mind*, lining your thinking up with the Word of God. We should always ask, "What does God's Word have to say about such-and-such? What does the Word say about me? What does the Word say that I have? What does the Word say that I am? What do I need to do now?" We need to say what God says. We need to agree with God.

Second Corinthians 5:17 says you become a new creature *in Christ*, but Ephesians 4:24 says, *...put on the new man....* There is something we need to do to put on the new man. Why? Because the new man is who you are on the inside and who you are *in Christ*. Paul is saying, "Take what you are and what you have *in Christ* and put it on." How do you put on the new man? By renewing your mind with God's Word.

Paul also says in verse 24 of Ephesians 4 that the new man ...*is created in righteousness and true holiness.* In other words, you are not trying to make the new man righteous and holy. He is saying, "The moment you are born again, you are a new creation, and you are created in righteousness and true holiness." Then he says, "...put on the new man...." Since you have been made a partaker of the divine nature, you are to put on the new man, who is created in righteousness and true holiness.

DETHRONE YOUR REASONING AND BODY

So what do you need to do? You don't need to make the new man righteous, but you need to *put him on.* How do you do that? *That the communication of thy faith may become effectual by the acknowledging of every good thing which is in you in Christ Jesus* (Philemon 6).

What would happen if you made a list and started acknowledging every good thing that is yours *in Christ?* God already deposited "every good thing" in you when you were born again, but it is up to you to *acknowledge* what you have *in Christ.*

You must acknowledge who you are and what you have *in Christ.* Just because you are a believer doesn't mean you won't have any trouble with your flesh or your mind. Even as a born-again, Spirit-filled believer, you still have to do something with your body. What did Paul say he did with his body? "...I keep under my body, and bring it into subjection..." (1 Corinthians 9:27).

God is not going to do anything about your body or your mind. He already did the biggest work in your spirit (your inward man) when you were born again. God gave you His Word, which is full of life and power, and the Holy Ghost lives on the inside of you.

You can do something with your body. Begin by acknowledging who you are *in Christ,* and let the Holy Ghost rise up on the inside of you. When you agree with God, your inner man (your spirit) will rise up and dethrone the dominance of your body and your reasoning.

THE ENGRAFTED WORD

In speaking to believers, James said, *Wherefore lay apart all filthiness and superfluity of naughtiness, and receive with meekness the engrafted word, which is able to save your souls* (James 1:21). Even after you are born again, you still have to get your soul saved. Your soul is made up of your mind, will, and emotions. That may sound like a contradiction; however, the newborn child of God must have a continual renewing of the mind. Paul says in Romans 12:1,2:

I beseech you therefore, brethren, by the mercies of God, that ye present your bodies a living sacrifice, holy, acceptable unto God, which is your reasonable service.

And be not conformed to this world: but be ye transformed by the renewing of your mind, that ye may prove what is that good, and acceptable, and perfect, will of God.

James says to receive the Word with meekness means to receive it with humility. In other words, humble yourself and be teachable. The engrafted Word has the ability to save, deliver, restore, and make your soul (your mind, will, and emotions) whole.

Why does James call the Word "the engrafted Word"? The Word doesn't work unless it is *implanted*. It won't work for you unless it is implanted on the inside of you. How do you get it implanted? *By acknowledging every good thing that is in you in Christ*. In other words, you stick with it and keep feeding and meditating on the Word.

FAITH IS AN ACT

In verse 22, James says, *But be ye doers of the word, and not hearers only, deceiving your own selves.* What does it mean to be a *doer of the Word*? When you see something in the Word, you just act on it. You start acting like the Word is true. You become a doer of that Word. If the Word says something belongs to you, you can say, "I am going to act on it. I am going to act like it is so. It may not feel like it or look like it, but I am acting on it *right now.*"

Smith Wigglesworth said, "Faith is an act." James said, *Faith without works [or corresponding action] is dead* (James 2:26). As you acknowledge the Word, start acting like it is true.

James 1:23,24 says:

For if any be a hearer of the word, and not a doer, he is like unto a man beholding his natural face in a glass [or in a mirror]:

For he beholdeth himself, and goeth his way, and straightway forgetteth what manner of man he was.

What do you look at when you look in the mirror? You look at yourself. James is saying, "If you hear the Word, but you don't do it, it is like looking in the mirror, going your way and forgetting what you look like."

Verse 25 says, *But whoso looketh into the perfect law of liberty, and continueth therein, he being not a forgetful hearer, but a doer of the work, this man shall be blessed in his deed.*

SEE YOURSELF IN CHRIST

How do you become a doer of the Word? You look into the mirror of the Word, which James calls "the perfect law of liberty."

When you get up in the morning, look up about ten *in Christ* Scriptures, look in the mirror, and acknowledge them. Look in the mirror, the perfect law of liberty. When you look into the mirror of the Word, it will make you free. One translation says, "Look and keep on looking."

When you keep on looking, there is a reflection and you see yourself *in Christ.* You see what God has done for you *in Christ,* and suddenly you see yourself free. You won't possess any more than you can see. If you continue to see yourself as a failure, unrighteous, unworthy, defeated, and confused, you will continue to live it out.

God can tell you over and over what He has done for you *in Christ* and who you are *in Christ,* but as long as you continue to see yourself as a failure, unrighteous, unworthy, defeated, sick, or poor, you will stay in that condition. While you go by your thinking and feelings, God is saying, "Acknowledge every good thing that is in you *in Christ.* Renew your mind and put on the new man, created in righteousness, victory, blessing, and holiness."

When you get up in the morning, look in the Word. When you have a lunch break, open your Bible. If you have a fifteen-minute break, open your Bible. This is what it takes to be blessed.

EVERYTHING WE NEED

God has deposited everything in you, through His Word, that you will ever need for life and godliness.

Second Peter 1:3 says, *According as his divine power hath given unto us all things....* If you need an answer, I will tell you where it is: "...his divine power hath given unto us *all things* that pertain unto life and godliness...." He didn't say you have been given all things that pertain to heaven. No, you have been given all things that pertain to life and godliness *right now* and "...through the knowledge of him that that called us to glory and virtue: Whereby are given unto us exceeding great and precious promises: that by these ye might be partakers of the divine nature, having escaped the corruption that is in this world through lust."

Peter is saying, "God has given you everything you need for life and godliness in the Word." James said, "You need to take these exceeding great and precious promises and get them engrafted on the inside of you. These promises will save your soul."

David the psalmist said, *Thy word have I hid in mine heart, that I might not sin against thee* (Psalm 119:11). In other words, the more of the Word you have in you, the less trouble you will have with sin.

To give mental assent to the Word won't work. James said for the Word to work for you, you need to lay aside all filthiness and superfluity of naughtiness. If you have 50 percent Word and 50 percent filthiness and superfluity of naughtiness, the Word won't work for you. It will have some effect, but you need to get 100 percent of the Word into you.

THE WORD WORKS

If you keep looking into the Word, it will save, deliver, heal, and restore your soul. It will bring the blessing of God. Acknowledge who you are and what you have *in Christ*.

Hebrews 4:12 says:

For the word of God is quick, and powerful, and sharper than any two-edged sword, piercing even to the dividing asunder of soul and spirit, and of the joints and marrow, and is a discerner of the thoughts and intents of the heart.

Nothing can separate your soul and your spirit but the Word. You ask, "Why do they need to be separated?" God says you are a new creature *in Christ*. He says you have been made righteous, and you are triumphant, but your mind is in disagreement. Your circumstances are in disagreement. Your feelings are in disagreement. But the Word is like a sharp sword. It will cause your circumstances and feelings to agree with God.

Jesus said, *Think not that I am come to send peace on earth: I came not to send peace, but a sword* (Matthew 10:34). The sword will reach into your soul and separate and cut things out that are hindering you from fulfilling the Word of God and being blessed.

Ephesians 6:17 talks about "...the sword of the Spirit, which is the word of God." The Word will cut controlling influences off of your life and things out of your soul that are not in agreement with God's Word.

What happens when you begin to acknowledge, "I am who God says I am. God says that I am an overcomer, so I say I am an overcomer. God says I have been made righteous, so I say right now, I am the righteousness of God *in Christ*"? The sword of the Spirit cuts controlling influences from your life.

REASON TO SHOUT

Numbers 23:19 says:

God is not a man, that he should lie; neither the son of man, that he should repent: hath he said, and shall he not do it? or hath he spoken, and shall he not make it good?

There is no way God can lie. If you find out what the Word says and you receive the engrafted Word, God will perform it in your life.

Numbers 23:20,21 says:

Behold, I have received commandment to bless: and he hath blessed; and I cannot reverse it.

He hath not beheld iniquity in Jacob, neither hath he seen perverseness in Israel: the Lord his God is with him, and the shout of a king is among them.

Once you know your covenant and who you are *in Christ*, there will be the shout of a king! If the Israelites were shouting under the Old Covenant, you have even more to shout about in the New Covenant. Just as God looked at the Israelites in the Old Covenant, He looks at you *in Christ*. He sees you as the righteousness of Christ. Balaam got a glimpse of the people the way God saw them. He didn't see iniquity in them.

What does this mean to you? If you have been made the righteousness of God *in Christ*, God sees no iniquity in you. You have reason to shout! It's time to get the Bible out and say, "Devil, if you can't read, let me read to you!"

The communication of your faith will become effectual as *you acknowledge every good thing that is in you in Christ!* Hallelujah!

WHAT YOU HAVE NOW IN CHRIST

God is planting a whole new crop of righteousness, wisdom, Redemption, sanctification, blessing, joy, and victory on the inside of you.

Put on the new man by declaring who you are *in Christ.* Make this confession of faith and acknowledge some of the things you have now "*in Christ*":

I am who God says I am. I have what God says I have. I acknowledge right now by faith every good thing that is mine in Christ. I am a new creation in Christ. Old things are passed away. A whole new world has opened up to me in Christ in the Spirit. I have been born again. I have been born of God. Old habits, attitudes, and controlling influences are broken and cut away from my life by the sword of the Spirit, which is the Word of God.

I acknowledge every good thing that is mine in Christ right now. I have been made the righteousness of God in Christ. Victory is mine now in Christ. In Him I am more than a conqueror. I have been refathered. God is my Father. I am righteous. I am strong in the Lord and in the power of His might.

I have been redeemed from the curse of the law. Christ has redeemed me from all iniquity. The law of the Spirit of life in Christ has made me free from the law of sin and death. I am free. I am righteous. Right now I am victorious. I am in Christ, and Christ is in me. I am blessed with every spiritual blessing in Christ right now. I am the workmanship of God, created in Christ Jesus. I receive with meekness the engrafted Word, which is saving my soul. I am a doer of the Word.

I am who God says I am. I am complete in Christ. In Him I am strong. In Him I am free. In Him I am blessed!

IN CHRIST SCRIPTURES
Who You Are and What You Have In Christ

IN CHRIST

Romans 3:24
Romans 8:1
Romans 8:2
Romans 12:5
1 Cor. 1:2
1 Cor. 1:30
1 Cor. 15:22
2 Cor. 1:21
2 Cor. 2:14
2 Cor. 3:14
2 Cor. 5:17

2 Cor. 5:19
Gal. 2:4
Gal. 3:26
Gal. 3:28
Gal 6:15
Eph. 1:3
Eph. 1:10
Eph. 2:6
Eph. 2:10
Eph. 2:13
Eph. 3:6
Phil. 3:13. 14

Col. 1:28
1 Thess. 4:16
1 Thess. 5:18
1 Tim. 1:14
2 Tim. 1:9
2 Tim. 1:13
2 Tim. 2:1
2 Tim. 2:10
2 Tim. 3:15
Phile. 1:6
2 Peter 1:8
2 John 1:9

IN HIM

Acts 17:28
John 1:4
John 3:15,16
2 Cor. 1:20
2 Cor. 5:21
Eph. 1:4
Eph. 1:10

Phil. 3:9
Col. 2:6
Col. 2:7
Col. 2:10
1 John 2:5
1 John 2:6
1 John 2:8
1 John 2:27

1 John 2:28
1 John 3:3
1 John 3:5
1 John 3:6
1 John 3:24
1 John 4:13
1 John 5:14,15
1 John 5:20

REFERENCES

Note: Scripture quotations are *King James Version,* unless otherwise marked. Some scripture quotations are the author's paraphrase.

Adams, Jay E. *The New Testament in Everyday English.* Baker Book House, Grand Rapids, Michigan, 1979.

Amplified Bible. Zondervan Publishing House, Grand Rapids, Michigan, 1972.

American Standard Version. Thomas Nelson and Sons, New York, New York, 1901.

Barclay, William. *The New Testament A New Translation.* Collins, London, England, 1968.

Barth, Markus. *Anchor Bible.* Double Day and Company, Inc., Garden City, New York, 1974.

Beck, William. *The Holy Bible In The Language of Today.* A. J. Holman Company, New York, New York, 1976.

Cressman, A. *Good News for the World.* SOON! Publications, Bombay, India, 1969.

Goodspeed, Edgar J., *The New Testament, An American Translation.* University of Chicago, Chicago, Illinois, 1923.

Hayman, Henry, *Four Volume Series, Letters of Apostle Paul.* Spirit to Spirit Publications, Tulsa, Oklahoma, 1982.

Jordan, Clarence. *The Cotton Patch Version of Paul's Epistles.* Association Press, New York, New York, 1968.

Laubach, Frank C. *The Inspired Letters in Clearest English.* Thomas Nelson and Sons, New York, New York, 1956.

Moffatt, James. *The Holy Bible Containing the Old and New Testaments.* Double Day and Company, Inc., Garden City, New York, 1926.

New American Standard Bible. A. J. Holman, New York, New York, 1971.

New English Bible. Oxford University Press, Oxford, England, 1961.

Noli, Fan. S. *The New Testament of Our Lord and Savior Jesus Christ.* Albanian Orthodox Church In America, Boston, Massachusetts, 1961.

Norlie, Olaf M. *Norlie's Simplified New Testament in Plain English — For Today's Readers.* Zondervan Publishing House, Grand Rapids Michigan, 1961.

Phillips, J.B. *The New Testament in Modern English*. The Macmillan Company, New York, New York, 1958.

Revised Standard Bible. Thomas Nelson and Sons, New York, New York, 1953.

Rotherham, J.B. *The Emphasized Bible*. Kregel Publications, Grand Rapids, Michigan, 1976.

Taylor Ken. *The Living Bible*. Tyndale House Publishers, Inc., Wheaton, Illinois, 1971.

The Distilled Bible/New Testament. Paul Benjamin Publishing Company, Stone Mountain, Georgia, 1980.

The Holy Bible, New International Version. Zondervan Publishing House, Grand Rapids, Michigan, 1978.

The Jerusalem Bible. Double Day and Company, Inc., Garden City, New York, 1968.

The New Testament English Version for the Deaf. Baker Book House, Grand Rapids, Michigan, 1978.

The Translator's New Testament. The British and Foreign Bible Society, London, England, 1977.

The Twentieth Century New Testament. Revised Edition. The Fleming H. Revell Company, New York, New York, 1909.

Verkuyl, Gerrit. *The Holy Bible, The New Berkeley Version, Revised Edition in Modern English*. Zondervan Publishing House, Grand Rapids, Michigan, 1969.

Way, Arthur S. *The Letters of St. Paul to the Seven Churches and Three Friends with the Letter to the Hebrews*. Sixth Edition. Macmillan and Company, New York, New York, 1926.

Weymouth, Richard Francis, *The New Testament*. James Clark and Company, London, England, 1909.

Williams, Charles G. *The New Testament*. Moody Press, Chicago, Illinois, 1978.

Williams, Charles Kingsley: *The New Testament, A New Translation in Plain English*. Longmans, Green, and Co., London, England, 1952.

In Christ

TAPE LIBRARY

12 TAPE SERIES

PAUL'S SYSTEM OF TRUTH ***$50.00***

In Apostle Paul's letters to the church, there is a network of revelation concerning who Christ is, what He has done for us, and who we are in Christ. The eight points to this system are:

1. WHAT IS MAN — SPIRIT, SOUL, BODY
2. IDENTIFICATION WITH ADAM
3. MAN'S CONDITION IN ADAM
4. WHAT HAPPENED TO JESUS FROM THE CROSS TO THE THRONE
5. IDENTIFICATION WITH CHRIST
6. WHO WE ARE AND WHAT WE HAVE NOW IN CHRIST
7. WHAT JESUS IS DOING FOR US NOW
8. HOW TO GROW UP IN CHRIST

8 TAPE SERIES

IDENTIFICATION WITH CHRIST ***$40.00***

"I am crucified with Christ: nevertheless I live; yet not I, but Christ liveth in me: and the life which I now live in the flesh I live by the faith of the Son of God, who loved me, and gave himself for me." Galatians 2:20

1. BEING "IN CHRISTED"
2. A MAN IN CHRIST
3. IN UNION WITH CHRIST
4. TWINNED WITH CHRIST
5. GOD'S GENETIC ENGINEERING
6. PUT OFF AND PUT ON
7. MADE ALIVE WITH CHRIST
8. IN CHRIST — IN THE ANOINTED ONE

THE LIFE OF PAUL ***$40.00***

The resurrected Christ appeared to Paul on the road to Damascus. The revelation of the Lord Jesus changed not only Paul's life, but the course of history has been greatly affected by Paul's obedience to the "Heavenly Vision."

1. THE RESURRECTION REALITY
2. PAUL - "THE HAPPY MAN"
3. PAUL'S PREPARATION - "UNIVERSITY OF ARABIA"
4. JOURNEY ONE - "REVIVALS AND RIOTS"
5. JOURNEY ONE - "GOSPEL DEMONSTRATION"
6. JOURNEY TWO (EUROPE) - "TURNING POINTS IN HISTORY"
7. JOURNEY THREE (ASIA) - "MIGHTILY GREW THE WORD"
8. JOURNEY THREE - "FINISH THE COURSE"

6 TAPE SERIES

GOD'S RESERVOIR OF ABUNDANCE........................... $30.00
"It seems there is an invisible reservoir of abundance in the universe that can be tapped by obeying certain spiritual laws." Norman Vincent Peale
1. GOD'S RESERVOIR OF ABUNDANCE
2. OVER AND ABOVE GIVING
3. OBEDIENCE AND FAITH IN GIVING
4. POSSESSING DOUBLE
5. CATCHING THE SPIRIT OF PROSPERITY
6. PROSPERITY AND HEALTH

4 TAPE SERIES

PREACHING THE GOSPEL I $20.00
Four favorite messages by Mark Hankins:
1. ARRESTED BY GOD
2. PIT PRAYERS, PROMISES, PROCLAMATIONS
3. WHY KINGS SHOUT
4. KEEP YOUR CONFIDENCE. . .CAST YOUR CARES

PREACHING THE GOSPEL II $20.00
Contains four faith messages:
1. FAITH/THE MEETING PLACE
2. FAITH/THE ROAD FOR SUPERNATURAL SUPPLY
3. MIXING FAITH WITH THE WORD
4. STRONG IN FAITH

THE BLOOD OF JESUS....................................... $20.00
Filled with the Spirit:
1. FAITH IN THE BLOOD
2. THE BLOOD: PAST, PRESENT & FUTURE
3. THE BENEFITS OF THE BLOOD
4. BOLDNESS BY THE BLOOD

THE LANGUAGE OF REDEMPTION $20.00
In Paul's revelation there is a language with certain terms and certain tenses that must be understood to produce freedom and release the power of God in our lives.
1. THE GOSPEL - "THE MESSAGE OF FREEDOM"
2. FIRST CLASS RIGHTEOUSNESS
3. JESUS SECURED OUR PERMANENT DELIVERANCE
4. SUPERNATURAL WORDS CONTAIN SUPERNATURAL POWER

FRAMING YOUR WORLD WITH THE WORD OF GOD............... **$20.00**
"If you knew what was on the other side of your mountain, you would move it."
1. WHAT'S HIDDEN IN THE QUARKS?
2. YOUR MOUNTAIN NEEDS TO HEAR YOUR VOICE
3. HEARING TO HEALING
4. YOUR FAITH IS A REFLECTION OF GOD

POSSESSING DOUBLE...................................... **$20.00**
"...When they had gone over, Elijah said to Elisha, Ask what I shall do for you before I am taken from you. And Elisha said, I pray you, let a double portion of your spirit be upon me." 2 Kings 2:9 (AMP)
1. POSSESSING DOUBLE
2. SUPERNATURAL INCREASE
3. CASTING SEED ON THE WATER
4. TAPPING GOD'S ABILITY

3 TAPE SERIES

CHRIST HATH REDEEMED US.................................. **$15.00**
"Neither by the blood of goats and calves, but by his own blood he entered in once in to the holy place, having obtained eternal redemption for us." Hebrews 9:12
1. "A COMPLETE REDEMPTION," EVERYTHING YOU NEED
2. THE LANGUAGE OF REDEMPTION
3. LEGALLY RELEASED, THE PRISON DOOR IS OPEN

THE PREVAILING POWER OF GOD'S WORD.................... **$15.00**
The centurion said to Jesus, "Speak the word only; and my servant shall be healed!" Jesus marveled at his faith. The Word arrived before the centurion got home and his servant was healed. Matthew 8:8 *(3 Tapes)*

SEEING THE UNSEEN...................................... **$15.00**
"While we look not at the things which are seen, but at the things which are not seen: for the things which are seen are temporal; but the things which are not seen are eternal." 2 Corinthians 4:18
1. BREAKING THE "SEEN" BARRIER
2. UNSEEN REALITIES
3. UNSEEN REALM AND THE HOLY SPIRIT

GLORY TO GLORY.. **$15.00**
"But we all, with open face beholding as in a glass the glory of the Lord, are changed into the same image from glory to glory, even as by the Spirit of the Lord." 2 Corinthians 3:18
1. THE GOSPEL, THE GLORY, AND THE HOLY SPIRIT
2. GLORY TO GLORY
3. NOTHING BUT GOD

THE HOLY GHOST FELL $15.00

The book of Acts is more than just a history book of the early church, it is the pattern for the move of God in every generation. The Holy Ghost not only satisfies us continually, but also enables us for World Harvest. In a dry and thirsty land, there is joy, healing, victory and blessing in the water of the Holy Spirit.

1. COME AND DRINK
2. THE FLOW OF THE HOLY GHOST (PART I)
3. THE FLOW OF THE HOLY GHOST (PART II)

THE ANCIENT PATHS $15.00

This generation of believers must be clearly instructed in the ways of the Lord. Many times it is easier to take the road of least resistance or the most comfortable path, but that will not bring the glory of God into our lives.

1. THE ANCIENT PATHS
2. SHOW ME THY WAY
3. GOD'S DOING NEW THINGS IN THE SAME OLD WAY

THE BALM OF GILEAD $15.00

The word "Gilead" means "perpetual spring." There is a continual flow of God's healing and restoration in Gilead. The Doctor is in and the medicine is free!

1. THE DOCTOR IS IN
2. BALM OF GILEAD
3. PERPETUAL SPRING

THE PROCESS OF CHANGE $15.00

It takes some changes to get the glory, but it takes the glory to get some changes. God wants you to move out of your ability and results into His ability and results.

1. LAUNCH OUT INTO THE DEEP
2. THE GLORY PRODUCES CHANGE
3. I HEAR THE SOUND OF THE RAIN

THE FIRE AND MOVE OF GOD $15.00

"If I say, I will not make mention of the Lord or speak any more in His name, in my mind and heart it is as if there were a burning fire shut up in my bones...." Jeremiah 20:9

1. THE FIRE AND THE MOVE OF GOD
2. NOW IS THE TIME, THIS IS THE PLACE, WE ARE THE PEOPLE
3. GOD'S RIGHTEOUS CAUSE AND PROSPERITY

UNLIMITED POSSIBILITIES $15.00

We need to spiritually remove the speed limits, get out of the broken down vehicle of doubt and unbelief, get in a "Holy Ghost Lexus" of faith, and remove the speed limit signs!

1. MOVE TO MONTANA
2. FUNDAMENTALS OF FAITH
3. MOUNTAIN MOVING FAITH

THE POWER OF WORDS **$15.00**
God framed this world by words; therefore, we frame our world by words.
1. THE POWER OF WORDS
2. FAITH-FILLED WORDS
3. LIVING BY FAITH

UNDERSTANDING WHO YOU ARE IN CHRIST **$15.00**
Once you understand your identity in Christ, never again will you identify with
defeat, failure, depression, sickness or lack.
1. FINDING YOUR PLACE IN THE ROCK
2. IDENTIFICATION WITH CHRIST
3. ACKNOWLEDGE WHAT YOU HAVE IN CHRIST

THE YEAR OF JUBILEE **$15.00**
This is the day "to proclaim the accepted and acceptable year of the Lord. [the day
when salvation and free favors of God profusely abound.]" Luke 4:19
1. THE YEAR OF JUBILEE
2. THE FIRE OF GOD BURNING
3. RAIN ON THE DESERT

TURNAROUND TIME! **$15.00**
You can mark your calendar when God gives you His Word. Mark the day and the
spot...Things are turning around.
1. A CALL FROM TOMORROW
2. FROM THIS DAY I WILL BLESS YOU
3. TIME FOR A TURNAROUND

FINDING YOUR COMPANY **$15.00**
There are important things you need to know that the Lord will not tell you...
But if He has told it to somebody you're supposed to be in relationship with, you'll
have to get it from them.
1. FINDING YOUR COMPANY
2. A VESSEL OF HONOR
3. SUPERNATURAL RELATIONSHIPS

THE SPIRIT OF FAITH **$15.00**
You can mark your calendar when God gives you His Word. Mark the day and the
spot...Things are turning around.
1. THE SPIRIT OF FAITH
2. YOUR MOUNTAIN NEEDS TO HEAR YOUR VOICE
3. YOUR VOICE IS YOUR ADDRESS

1-800-555-2757

WHEN HE SAW THEIR FAITH.................................**$15.00**
The hole you knock from the natural to the supernatural opens the way for you to enter the presence of Jesus and also makes a way for others to jump through the same hole.
1. JESUS SAW THEIR FAITH
2. THE CRY OF FAITH
3. JUBILEE FAITH

MAKING MONEY MOVE......................................**$15.00**
"...thou broughtest us out into a wealthy place" (Psalm 66:12). Money's moving, money's shaking, strongholds are breaking.
1. MONEY IS MOVING
2. TAKING THE LIMITS OFF OF GOD
3. HAVING A MONEY MINISTRY

BOOKS & STUDY MANUALS

SPIRIT-FILLED SCRIPTURE STUDY GUIDE........................ $25.00
Informative and inspirational study guide packed with over 100 translations.

PAUL'S SYSTEM OF TRUTH.................................... $25.00
In Paul's letters to the church, there is a network of revelation concerning who Christ is, what He has done for us, and who we are in Christ.

TAKING YOUR PLACE IN CHRIST............................... $7.00
Understanding Your Identity and Inheritance In Him.

THE POWER OF IDENTIFICATION WITH CHRIST.................. $10.00
In Christ, the power and grace of God reversed the condition Satan had caused in mankind and is released through your identification with Christ.

MUSIC

BE IT UNTO ME — BY TRINA HANKINS
With God nothing is impossible of fulfillment.
Tape $10.00
CD.. $15.00

A PLACE BY THE FATHER — BY TRINA HANKINS
There is a place by the Father and that place is in Christ Jesus.
Tape $10.00
CD.. $15.00

Mark Hankins Ministries

Mark and Trina Hankins

MARK AND TRINA HANKINS are the pastors of Christian Worship Center in Alexandria, Louisiana. Pastor Hankins is the founder of In Christ International Bible School and also has a daily television ministry program called *Rejoice*. Pastor Hankins' radio program, *Taking Your Place in Christ,* is heard in many parts of the United States. Trina, an anointed praise and worship leader, has also recorded a second album, *Be It Unto Me.*

Prior to their pastorate, Mark Hankins was an evangelist who traveled extensively with his family throughout the United States and overseas conducting revivals, seminars, and campmeetings.

Pastor Hankins still travels nationally and internationally throughout the world preaching the Word of God with the Holy Ghost. His message centers on Redemption in Christ and who the believer is "In Christ."

ORDER FORM

Please clip and return to: Mark Hankins Ministries
P.O. Box 12863 • Alexandria, LA 71315

Name _____

Address _____

City _____ State/Zip _____

Telephone _____

QTY.	DESCRIPTION	UNIT PRICE	AMOUNT
	Shipping & Handling	1-3 items — $3.00	
		4-6 items — $5.00	
		TOTAL ENCLOSED	